MW00614667

SECOND EDITION

ISBN 978-0-578-67321-9

www.thinkgetagrip.com

Table of Contents

DISCLAIMER

Before we get started, I must lay out the fact that this book is intended to provide general information on mindset. I am not providing any legal or professional advice. In fact, the statements made here are only my opinions and should not be understood to be medical, psychological, or any other advice. If you feel you need professional assistance, you must seek advice from the appropriate licensed professional. This book does not provide complete information on the subject matter covered. This book is not intended to address specific requirements, either for an individual or an organization. This book is intended to be used only as a general guide, and not as a sole source of information on the subject matter. While I have undertaken diligent efforts to ensure every detail is as it should be, there is no guarantee of accuracy or of no errors, omissions or typographical errors. Any slights of people or organizations are unintentional. Any reference to any person or organization whether living or dead is purely storytelling. The author and publisher shall have no liability or responsibility to any person or entity and hereby disclaim all liability, including without limitation, liability for consequential damages regarding any claim, loss or damage that may be incurred, or alleged to have been incurred, directly or indirectly, arising out of the information provided in this book.

Now with that out of the way let's get started.

I.   THE START TO THINKING

The mind is not a vessel to be filled, but
a fire to be kindled.
Plutarch

When I try to recall my earliest memory, I remember my mother making me give a pair of shorts to a neighbor girl, who I played with, when I was around three years old. (for the life of me I can't remember her name) That is my first big memory. And it was imprinted in my brain because those were my fav shorts and my mother made me give them to her. Looking back now I realize I likely had outgrown them, and they were perfectly good shorts to be used by someone else. But the real reason this was such a big memory is that when this neighbor girl and I were in the sandbox playing, she peed in them, in my favorite shorts!

Now as a grownup do you think I like to share my clothes?

We all have such "short" stories that impact who we are. These stories are our memories that form our character and drive in life. These memories are often random and the reason we have them is unclear.

I have a memory of a teeny tiny girl who my elementary principal took special care of. I can clearly recall seeing this little waif standing next to my larger-than-life principal (whom I adored but was afraid of too) to get her hair combed each morning. I can recall being confused by the fact that she got special treatment, and I didn't learn until later that she and her family were in need of a lot of help.

Then I remember Rex, an elementary memory too. On the days he came to school, and that wasn't every day, he always had sleep goobers in his eyes and nasty crusty boogers caked on his nose. He was out of control most days which during my upbringing was highly unusual. At the time I gave none of this too much thought. I didn't know who he was, or what he needed. And I think during that time not much was done to teach kids how to think or rise above their situation. This bothers me now but back then it didn't.

Rex and the little girl were added to my list of "short" stories.

Fast forward to middle school. Most days were the same. But in May of my 7th grade year there was a mine disaster and 91 men died. The mine caught fire and the men couldn't get out. So many children lost their dads that day. We lived in a small mining town and were a close-knit community and that hit hard. I didn't totally understand it all, but I can clearly recall the eerie feeling and how sad everyone was. No one saw that coming and when it hit, it was devastating. Was counseling offered to those in need? What was done to help them navigate such a huge loss?

During those same middle school years, an upper grade girl got pregnant and was sent to, wait for it, ... The Home For Wayward Mothers. I am not joking, that was the name. Females were not allowed to remain in school when they were in a family way (another way of saying pregnant in those days). And in grade nine one of our own classmates got pregnant and I think she was relegated to her house. I never saw her until after she had given birth, and I assume, someone had adopted the baby. Now I wonder who helped these young girls deal with their emotions.

How hard was that for them? How did they make it through?

Then came high school, dances, boys, crushes, parties, etc. And during those formative years, I didn't ask anyone for clarification, I just made-up reasons for things and learned on the go. I watched many of my classmates do things that weren't good, or nice, or safe. I know they too were struggling with thoughts and worries but none of us were taught how to deal.

And finally, I went to university where I met many wonderful new friends. One of them was so nice, so handsome, and so in need of a friend. He had come home from Vietnam to find his wife in love with his best friend. We talked a lot about how hurt he was. But I didn't understand just how in need he was until I got the call that he had killed himself. I was totally confused, so sad, didn't know how or who to talk to about this, and I certainly didn't understand how mental wellness worked.

Over the years I have experienced a few such early ended lives which today still fill me with sadness. Patrick was another. He was terribly depressed, such a talented wonderful human, yet saw no other alternative than to end his life. There was a set of twins, in their youth, fooling around while driving when after a fight one decided to show the other and purposefully fell out of the car. Because of how he landed he was dead on impact. His brother lasted a year and then ended his own life because he just couldn't take the guilt of it anymore. I could list several others, all of which have impacted me and are part of my "short" stories.

These are just a few of the major memories I can recall from my own youth. I have seen messy lives while growing up, experienced many more with those I have worked with, and lived some of them with dear friends as an adult. Mine has been messy too. I believe all lives are. But do we teach how to handle our emotions and make good decisions?

I have witnessed students hack into the school grading system to change their grades because they were sure that would gain them entrance into the university they thought they needed to go to. Not understanding the impact of their decision, they were totally surprised to be caught and suffer the consequences of their choice. I have received forged signatures and been lied to more times than I can count about the validity of where and with whom and what the kids were doing. These lies not only came from my students but their parents as well.

I have watched parents smother their children with close scrutiny, hovering over them, doing too much for their kids thereby sending the unintended message that they don't think their child is capable and implying their child can't live life without them. I have listened to children have hopes and dreams that they talk themselves out of for fear of failure. And I have watched children second guess their every move and believe they are not pretty enough, good enough, or smart enough to count. All of these are part of my memories and "short" stories.

Because of my "short" stories, I am driven to help. They instilled in me a desire to do what I can for others. Over my years I learned and developed coping strategies and thinking techniques which helped me and those in my life and profession to gain control, rise above, and live the life we desire and deserve.

But a couple of years ago a former colleague of mine ended her life. She was like the others who had done the same, beautiful, kind, loving, and so very sad. Hearing of her death made me decide enough is enough. And it was while talking and grieving together with one of my longtime friends and parent of children I have taught, that she asked what we could do to stop this pattern.

Thus, the idea and desire to write this book. It is as if my life has filled me with "short" stories so that I can offer help.

I wish I could turn back the clock for the people who are gone and help them know how important their lives are and how much we need them. I wish I knew then what I know now so that I could change the outcome. I did what I could to help my students rise above their fears and now, after so many experiences and lifelong learning, I know exactly how important it is for all of us to get a handle on how and what we think and learn to be well, spiritually, physically, and mentally, and do this as early as possible.

As I look back on all my ups and downs in life, all the things I have experienced and all the lessons I have been taught and learned, I feel fortunate that I have been able to cope and get through the tough spots and I am more than ever driven to help others to do the same.

And because I know what I know, and as a person who wants to help, I am hopeful I can help you and yours, and those you know, GET A GRIP on your mental wellness by the words I have written. Even if you are not the one in need, by reading this book you may be able to help others who are.

Take a moment right now to write down your first memories and think about how they impact who you are and what you are driven to do.

II. THE ORIGINS, IMPORTANCE OF, AND WHO AM I TO TEACH YOU HOW TO GET A GRIP

Recognize what you are thinking.
Direct your thoughts to those that are true
and work well and do this consistently.
Think what needs to be thought,
when it needs to be thought,
whether you want to or not.
This is what it means to
"GET A GRIP".
Heather Murray

It isn't easy to GET A GRIP. I won't lie to you about that, but it is the most important work you can do for yourself. Changing our thoughts is heavy lifting, but when we do, we change our perspective, gain a sense of happiness, and feel rock solid in life.

In my early years, I was often nervous, disappointed, frustrated, scared, embarrassed. I worried a lot, and I became a master of mad and sad. Like all kids, I didn't understand my feelings. People didn't talk about emotions other than to say things like, behave yourself, or stop crying. In my late teens, I suffered severe stomach aches and would double over with pain. My doctor told me it was the nerve endings from my back affecting my abdomen and suggested I lie quietly on my back till the pain subsided. It worked, so I didn't think too much about it and did not connect it to my tendency to worry and my lack of ability to deal with being anxious. In university I was filled with worry about what other people thought. In my early twenties as I started my career in education, I continued to worry, and many new emotions struck me. I loved working with high school students and took my duties to educate very seriously. I tried to be perfect in everything I did, and most especially wanted to do right by my students and be the best teacher ever. I worked long hours and was often consumed by my desire to be the best in everyone's eyes. Then in my mid-twenties, after my first-year teaching, I got married, and became an instant mother to two young, active girls. In the last year of my twenties, I was not only a mom to two stepdaughters, but I also had one toddler, and a newborn. Because of the enormity of all my duties, I was very scared, worried, and fearful that I would make big mistakes, maybe even do something so wrong that my children would die. I knew I had to GET A GRIP even though I didn't have a clue what I could hang onto.

For many years my life was overwhelming, because as a mother to a blended family of four, and a working mother and wife, many days I would wake up late, rush to be on time, and hope I had not forgotten the important details of all the schedules I was juggling. Once at work I would suffer the perceived jabs made by my boss and try to be my best.

But I never met the expectations for what I perceived others wanted from me. I would end each day super frustrated with my response to daily trials and tribulations.

At home, as the day drew to a close, I spent my alone time worrying about what I had done wrong, what I had said that wasn't "cool" and then tried to let it go which, by the way, never worked. As I aged, I realized this was my life pattern and wanted it to change.

I set out to learn all about dealing with my thoughts so I could handle my emotions and live the calm organized life I dreamed of. As I worked on my goal, I gleaned many lessons from each experience and role I played in my life. As I worked on handling my emotions, I learned and perfected several strategies to GET A GRIP, which I use to this very day. They work well for me and have worked equally well for everyone I have taught them to.

Knowing what I know, and therefore able to choose my thoughts, feelings, and actions, I can't stand idly by watching children and adults become overwhelmed. It has always gotten under my skin that we don't intentionally teach the fundamental skills of emotional intelligence during the 13 long years of school. And I am amazed that high school graduates are sent off to university and life with the expectation that they will be a top performer in every way while left to fend for themselves on the emotional field of life. In fact, it gets so far under my skin that I am like the movie characters in the 1976 film *Network* who stick their heads out of their house windows and yell at the top of their lungs, "I'm mad as hell, and I'm not going to take this anymore!"

To do something about this, I decided to teach how to think in terms of emotions. I took many courses and read many books and through all my experiences and learning, and with my own insight, which came from meeting my personal needs, I developed my strategies to GET A GRIP which involve changing what and how we think. I created the techniques in this book to retool thinking. I needed them in my own personal life, and I honed them in my profession to be useful to others.

I want to teach my GET A GRIP strategies to anyone and everyone who needs or wants them. Most especially, I want children to learn these techniques while they are young so they can reach their promise and potential and not have to wade through the muck of life or reinvent the proverbial wheel. I want them frontloaded to GET A GRIP. So, if you have children in your life, this book is for them too. Teach them as you learn.

WHAT IT MEANS TO GET A GRIP

Life can be exhilarating, and most times it is, but there are days which demand my best efforts. During these instances and experiences, it feels like life is handing out lemons and we are supposed to make lemonade. But, since we don't have all the ingredients or the recipe, we feel overwhelmed and respond with anger and/or frustration.

Early on as a teenager, when life got hard, I would say to myself, "Whatever," and let lots of things slide. But, as I aged and wanted to be a good human, a capable adult, and successful in life, I realized "whatever" wasn't going to cut it.

As I grew up, I became increasingly overcome by daily emotions and couldn't let things slide. Life created many experiences which required that I step up my game, and because of these "opportunities" for learning, I realized I had to do what needed to be done, when it needed to be done, whether I wanted to or not, to reach my own promise and potential.

When I became a teacher, my goal was to educate my students to be their best, and I did everything I could to help them on their way. But it wasn't until I became a mother that I truly understood the depth of my desire to teach the skills necessary to be our best and GET A GRIP.

Life is packed with situations and experiences that demand we step up to the plate, take a swing, and hit a home run. In other words, do what needs to be done, when it needs to be done, whether we want to or not. This is what I call "GET A GRIP". I am not sure when, from whom, or where I developed the saying, but "GET A GRIP" means I actually choose the thoughts I think because they are what control my emotions, which in turn impact my actions.

My one and only sister, older than I am, knows everything about me, and when I told her GET A GRIP was to be the title of this book she giggled and said it was perfect because that is what I have said my entire adult life. Over the years, saying "GET A

GRIP" to myself has pushed me to grab opportunities and saved me from despair.

Let me give you a prime example. Picture me as a young mother living in a foreign country just having locked my keys and my baby in the car. To set the stage, let's back up a bit as to why I ended up being in this foreign country in the first place.

My husband and I wanted to experience living abroad and the company he worked for had a location in Austria. Although we tried as newlyweds, my husband didn't get an overseas job offer until two years into our marriage when I was seven months pregnant. Being young and too confident for my own good, I thought it would be an easy thing to live in a foreign country as a new mother with a brand-new baby, so we gladly accepted and started to plan our move. We decided we would leave after our baby was born. Luckily, I knew myself well enough to know I needed to give birth in my country where I can understand the language spoken.

I can vividly recall rethinking our decision to move when our daughter was just one week old. I was sprawled on the floor alongside her in our completely empty master bedroom as the movers packed up the rest of our house. At that moment I realized I may have bitten off more than I could chew, but was too stubborn and proud to back out of my decision. In hindsight, I am glad I was able to forge ahead.

Once the house was packed, we lived in a hotel in our town for another week and then, knowing I would be far away and it would be difficult for my parents to come visit, I flew to New Mexico to stay with them. At the same time, my hubby flew overseas to work.

When our daughter was four weeks old, I left my parents and everything I had known and flew to Frankfurt (Germany) where my husband met us. We then flew on to Graz (Austria), drove to the small town of Lieboch, and moved into yet another hotel. It took a couple of weeks for us to move into our rental home and set up house. Every day I tried my best to feel normal, but being alone in a country I had never seen, a new mother not sure of herself, and not speaking one word of the language, I not only didn't feel normal, I felt completely lost.

It was the 1980s, things were different. There were no cell phones so you could easily call home. No GPS to guide driving. No social media to stay connected. And shopping was a whole new experience to say the least.

One big difference was the individual shops for different items. When I needed meat, I went to a butcher shop. One day I wanted to make something that reminded me of home, spaghetti and meatballs, so knowing I had to speak German, the national language used in Austria, I memorized the word for ground beef, faschiertes. This is an old-fashioned word but because we lived in a tiny old-fashioned town, that is what they used. It is not that easy to read, and even less easy to pronounce, but I worked hard to be able to do just that. When I arrived at the shop, I asked for faschiertes and was answered with a question that involved a word that sounded like raw. I was confused. Not only because I didn't speak German, but also because why on earth would I want to eat raw ground beef? Somehow, I finally thought to say spaghetti and that seemed to make sense to the butcher, and in short order she handed me a nicely wrapped parcel containing one pound of hamburger.

A year or so later I learned about beef tartare and the need for a fine cut of beef because it was eaten raw. Ah, that is why the butcher wanted to know if I wanted it raw or not.

Many instances like this unnerved me those first few weeks. I was in a constant state of unrest. When I wanted to buy chicken, which seems like an easy purchase, I was again caught off guard. I never would have guessed it came with the head and feet attached. I tried my best to sever the limbs and head, even tried covering it with a dish towel, but nothing helped, I just couldn't stomach doing it. I assured my husband we would never eat chicken again if this was how it would be.

Because of these experiences, I was certain I wouldn't be able to do any of the normal things I thought a mother should do.

Shop for groceries, cook or join a mom and me group. You name it, I was sure I would never do it.

The first weekend after moving into our house my husband tried to comfort me by talking me into exploring the area with our daughter. Anxious to feel "normal" I happily agreed. So, we all went on an outing to investigate the nearby city of Graz. After having a great time and seeing that it wasn't all that different from "home" I decided I could do this on my own with our baby.

As my daughter and I arrived in Graz, we parked in the same car park we used when there with my husband. Because technology had not yet arrived, with self-paid parking etc., there was a real person in the pay booth.

It was a splendid fall day and my daughter and I had a great time walking the streets of Graz. We all know babies follow a simple "routine" of eat, sleep, and well, you get the picture. Mine was no different, so when nature called, we returned to the car and I took care of business. When I finished feeding and cleaning her, I got out of the back seat, went around to the other side and put my darling girl in her safe and secure car seat. As I completed that task and started to close the door, an alarm went off in my head, but too late. The door clicked shut and I realized the doors were all locked, my purse was inside the car with the car keys along with my precious baby who, like all babies, hated the car seat and was crying.

Panic rose in my throat and although flight wanted to take hold, I was paralyzed with fear. And to top it all off my negative thoughts started to surface. "How dumb could I be?" "Can I do nothing right?" "Seriously, what is wrong with me?"

What was I to do? I wanted to give up, but I couldn't allow myself to sit down and cry.

At that moment I figuratively grabbed myself by the shirt collar and said these all-important words: GET A GRIP! I had to come up with a plan, and fast. This was not the time to freak out.

First, I ran to the woman attendant behind the glass and as she looked up, I tried to appear natural so I wouldn't scare her because the last thing I wanted to do was delay any possible solution by involving the police or something. And I needed her to listen while I acted out my dilemma.

With her staring at me, I placed my arms in the form of a cradle and rocked them back and forth as if I had a baby in them. Out loud, I said to her, "Baby?" She nodded.

Assuming she would understand wasn't a stretch since I had waved at her earlier as we exited for our outing. She had seen my sweet, tiny baby.

Then, I formed my hands in the 10 and 2 traditional steering wheel formation and pretended to drive and said, "Auto?" Again, the woman understood and nodded. Finally, I acted out keys in my hand and twisted my wrist as if starting a car with a key, and I said, "Keys?" Once again, she nodded, but with a bit of a puzzled look. Knowing she needed the full picture, I put it all together: baby, (she nods). Keys, (she nods). In (pointing down) auto. Hurrah!! Victory! She got it and had concern written all over her face. She promptly got on the phone and I knew she was calling someone to come and open the car, even though I couldn't understand one word coming out of her mouth.

As if I didn't have enough to deal with and what added another layer to my demise is that I don't usually travel with cash. I know, bad practice, and on this day, I had some, but not enough to pay someone to come open my car. I knew not everyone in Graz liked people who weren't local, or foreigners, although most did. Graz just didn't have many outside influences, so when the man arrived to open my door, I just looked scared and didn't speak. He saw my baby in the back seat and quickly went to work to open the door.

As he worked, I worried he might be mad when he realized I was a foreigner and couldn't pay him. I imagined him relocking the door when he discovered this truth. So, as he finished, I immediately rushed in and stood between the open door and the car, turned to him and said in English, "I am so sorry, I don't have money to pay you right now, but I will write down my address and when I receive the bill, I promise to send you a check right away." I smiled my best smile possible. He understood what I said and was clearly not pleased, but with no other choice, accepted my address and, as promised, when the bill arrived in the mail, I paid it promptly.

THOUGHTS CREATE FEELINGS AND ACTIONS

Learning to think well in the midst of a challenging situation such as the one I just told you about is the cornerstone of GET A GRIP. Thoughts control so much of who we are and how we perceive ourselves and the world around us. What we think becomes how we feel, which turns into the actions we take.

As I drove home from that parking garage in Graz, my mind immediately went to the dark side. I was shaken, scared, and completely overwhelmed. Feeling like this caused me to ruminate on how things could have gone wrong rather than celebrate that it all turned out well. My brain stayed negative. I felt like an idiot and worried I would never again be able to do things alone. As I worked through where I was mentally, I realized I had work to do on my mindset and how much I needed to control my worries, fears, and thoughts, recognize what I was thinking, and direct my thoughts to those that are true and work well, or simply, GET A GRIP.

These types of experiences taught me that much of what happens on a daily basis, when we least expect it, involves overwhelming emotions. Many demands of living, both large and small; separation, death, divorce, moving, sickness, being fired, app passwords, dropped calls, no WIFI, etc., ruffle our feathers and require that we control our thoughts. As I worked on getting a grip, I learned that many days I have to just push through. I learned that even though experiences can be scary, I can't stand like a deer in the headlights, blinded by the bright lights of fear. And finally, I learned that I can't wallow in regret – I must change my negative thinking. As a new mother, I committed myself to work on getting a grip on my mindset for my children.

Because we learn so much from what we see and hear as a child, I wanted to make sure, as their mother, that I could help my children develop every skill they needed to maintain their grip on life. To do that I knew I had to work on me first, and then use every lesson I could learn to teach them. And I needed to remember at any given moment they were watching my every move.

Now, as I watch my adult children live their lives, I can say with confidence that I did what I set out to do. I am thankful I helped them develop the mental skills they need to get a grip on their thoughts and emotions so they can tackle life. They have had children, experiences, work environments, divorces, illnesses, you name it, all of which presented challenges they had to work through. I am blessed to have children who are capable, good quality humans who have a grip.

HI, I AM HEATHER

Right about now you must be asking yourself who Heather Murray is to tell you how to do this for yourself and your children. Before I tell you about me, let me first say thank you for joining me and reading my book. I hope you enjoy what I have written and find it useful.

Hi, I'm Heather Murray and I want to introduce myself, so you know why I am able to tell you how to GET A GRIP.

I am a passionate educator who spent 38 successful years improving the mindset and educational accomplishments of 1000s of students. I not only taught students and counseled their parents, but trained colleagues as an administrator too.

I graduated from University with a Bachelor of Sciences degree in Education and a Master's in Mathematics. During the early part of my career, I taught math to students of all abilities. My happiest teaching moments were hearing a child say, "I get it!" Being good at math makes kids feel smart, and when my students learned they could be successful in a math class they not only felt smart, but they learned the value of staying the course and they realized the focus and effort it takes to accomplish something.

I spent time as a Dean of Students in middle school, guiding students and parents, and enjoyed teaching essential lifelong skills to all in my care. I loved helping young people learn how to reach their promise and potential.

Working in the capacity of Mathematics Department Chair for a Pre-K - 12 school I was able to institute systems of collaboration in teaching and grading that served students in math well.

As a Middle School Director and Elementary School Vice-Principal, I had the wonderful opportunity to plan and create educational programs that guided and inspired young people as they gained emotional and intellectual skills.

As the STEM leader at the Prek-12 school I was able to institute a STEM program that taught designing solutions for our modern world while connecting math, science, technology, and engineering to service.

I have had the good fortune to work with and learn from some of the finest school leaders, teachers, counselors, and world-class authors. It has been my honor to have been published in several magazines and blogs. I maintain my own website, raisinggoodhumans.com, which houses my parenting, school, and life related blog posts. I have consulted with schools to develop programs and schedules that best meet the needs of current learners and what their future will demand. I have been a School Life Coach who works with students and parents to help them navigate what it means to make the most of their years in school. I am on several social media platforms; FB, Instagram, and Twitter, posting often to support mental and emotional health. Sign up on my website and follow me on your favorite platform.

On a more personal note, I have experienced a lot of change in my life that has made me very flexible and outgoing. Moving and changing homes has been a big part of my journey in life. During my 39 years of marriage (and still counting), I have lived in three countries, four provinces and six states, now in Idaho. Over these 39 years, my hubbie and I have lived in more than 20 different homes (that I can recall). These moves are part of my life experiences that have "helped" me develop strategies for how to GET A GRIP.

But the most important aspect of who I am is that of being a mother to a blended family of three girls and one boy, and I proudly say they are all successful adults and good humans. Raising them is my greatest accomplishment and the most demanding thing I have ever attempted. It required that I bring my best and use every skill I have ever learned.

III. WHY AND HOW THE BOOK WORKS

*Emotional Intelligence: abilities such as being able
to motivate oneself and delay gratification; to
regulate one's moods and to keep distress from
swamping the abilities to think; to empathize and
to hope.*
Daniel Goleman

Have you ever experienced self-doubt, anxiety, demotivation, fear of failure or any of the other lovely emotional and mental challenges life throws at us? And responded in a way that didn't work well for you? Haven't we all?

Maintaining our positive emotions impacts all we do and this maintenance comes from managing our stream of consciousness. Think GET A GRIP is all about learning simple strategies that help us choose and think the thoughts that work well, feel better, and respond in the way we want.

Right now, I want you to analyze how many times per week you feel a sense of joy? When was the last time you belly laughed? How many hours per week do you spend doing something that you choose and you enjoy?

I imagine your answers to all these questions are very little. And I want to fix that so you can GET A GRIP, attain your goals, feel joy, and live the life you not only desire by deserve.

The study of raising good humans and the associated study of human psychology has occupied much of my life. I have always been interested in how humans tick. The intent of this book is to showcase the importance of having control of fear, worries, judgmental thoughts, and limiting beliefs so we can avoid being triggered and subsequently GET A GRIP on life.

AN EMOTIONAL INTELLIGENCE ROADMAP

This book is intended to be an instructional manual, a sort of emotional intelligence roadmap. It contains the summary and highlights of what I have learned and is written so you can "download" the information easily. Regardless of your personal experiences, you will be able to work toward improving your mindset and learn how to teach yourself, and those in your life, how to GET A GRIP. You will read my personal experiences which I offer so you can understand more thoroughly what I mean when I talk about the why, what, and how of getting a grip.

I start with how we think and what has influenced what we think about. After that we will move on to what type of thoughts stand in our way of getting a grip, how we can work through what hinders us, and how we can make GET A GRIP happen. I also include information on the process of changing thought habits and a method of tracking progress.

REACH YOUR PROMISE AND POTENTIAL

In order for us to reach our promise and potential and be better humans, spouses, students, employees, friends, and community members, we must maintain our thought process and learn to GET A Grip.

The exercises span either thirteen weeks or six. Each chapter is the description of one of the thirteen weeks along with a tracking progress sheet, journal page, and more in-depth tracking (if you want to do a deep dive).

You may know some of these topics, and others will be new. I recommend using the more in-depth tracking for the new learning and the less intense tracking for what you are familiar with.

Perhaps the first time through you can work on the less intense tracking and the second time through the more in depth, or vice versa.

The six-week schedule is in chapter XXII. You will follow the suggestions of what to do daily from the other chapters but topics are combined each week to accommodate the shortened time frame.

IV. WHAT, HOW, AND WHY WE THINK OUR THOUGHTS, AND WHAT INFLUENCES WHAT WE THINK ABOUT

*There is nothing either good or bad
but thinking makes it so.*
William Shakespeare

The act of thinking is both weird and fascinating. Have you ever wondered why on earth you are thinking the particular thoughts that are in your mind? During my waking hours and most of my sleeping ones too, I am constantly thinking, but I don't often wonder about how my brain works. I bet you are in the same boat.

THOUGHTS ARE MOSTLY JUST NOISE

Have you noticed that most of what you are thinking about has nothing to do with anything important? Do you realize your thoughts are just noise filling the void, not something that needs attention or work?

To help understand our thoughts, and how to control them to GET A GRIP, I have done some research and lots of reading.

SMELL TRIGGERS MEMORY

Thoughts can be ideas, memories, pictures, and music, and the smell of something can trigger a thought like nothing else. When I smell newly cut grass, my mind immediately goes to summer as a child and I feel relaxed and happy. Or if I smell Coppertone suntan lotion (what a funny combination of words from my youth, now we wear sunscreen) I remember in vivid detail the city pool where I spent countless summer hours swimming with my friends. As an adult, I have used the smell of Coppertone to help maintain my happy place during dark winter months. I rub some Coppertone on my skin, take a whiff, and sense summer is right around the corner.

Next time you catch the scent of some delicious smell, check in with your thoughts to see what was triggered in your memory bank.

THOUGHTS ARE CHEMICAL AND ELECTRICAL

How we think thoughts is based on the fact that thoughts are electrical and chemical processes in our brain. Because of our unique DNA, which dictates our chemical and electrical makeup, each of us thinks in our own special way. We have our own set of brain chemicals, or lack thereof, which greatly influence our outlook on life. But even though we are each unique, there is some commonality to how our brain works.

OUR BRAIN IS A PROCESSING MACHINE

Our brain processes our thoughts and tries to make sense out of what it takes in, all in an effort to make sure we can understand, function, and survive. My simple explanation of how this works goes like this; once a thought comes into our head, the brain sends it to memory to check to see if it already knows something about the thought and if it understands what to do. For example, you get the thought that you are hungry. The brain sends this to memory to check what you already know. If you are older, you remember what food is and what food you like. You also recall where food is stored, how to prepare food, and how much you want to eat. As a baby, you learn to scream to summon the person with food. So much easier, right?

If, on the other hand, you have a thought about something you know nothing about, the brain starts to analyze and seeks to understand. Once it does, or thinks it does (wink wink), it sends orders to execute. Because we didn't know anything about this new idea, the way we decide to act may or may not be good. But regardless, we do act and then store the outcome for future use.

Let's use learning to drive as an example. When we first get behind the wheel everything feels awkward and we are unsure of what to do. If you recently taught your teenager how to drive, you will know exactly what I mean. When, as a new driver we come to an intersection we are overwhelmed by the number of decisions we must make. And if we are turning left, heaven help us to do the right thing. But once we have driven a few times our mind starts to understand what is expected and how things work, or so we think. Maybe we lucked out, even though we did something wrong. We didn't have any problems the first few times, and due to the fact that things worked out, we stored the outcome for future use only to learn later that is not the right way to handle the situation. And after years of driving, we tend to take it all for granted. We think we can text or put on makeup while we drive and still be safe.

I can clearly recall my experience in driver's ed. Living in a small town I was with the driving instructor at the same time as two of my good friends. One friend was not what I would call mechanically inclined and she confused the gas pedal with the brake more times than I care to remember. It was scary, because the instructor didn't have one of those brake pedals on his side, and until she learned the different pedals on hers, our driving instructor was close to a heart attack each time she took the wheel. Thankfully, her brain eventually did fully process which pedal does what, but it was a long nine weeks to say the least.

THOUGHTS POP INTO OUR HEAD

Research explains that thoughts pop into our heads because of the stimuli around us, and that they are based on our conditioning. According to some of the brain gurus, our brain processes thoughts but does not actually create them. When I heard this, I was like, "What? Can that be true?" I struggled to believe this, but when I analyzed what happens as I drive, I had to agree that thoughts do pop into my mind.

When I am behind the wheel my mind goes on autopilot. It is full of me thinking, but not necessarily focused on the task at hand, which should be getting from point A to point B. I drift off to ideas like:

I must call Mom. When was the last time we talked? Yesterday? No, I think the day before. And I tell my car to dial "Roberta" (I had to change the voice prompt to her name because it couldn't detect what I was saying when I said mum).

Sue, I wonder how she is doing? She pops into my mind even though Sue is from my distant past, I don't see her because she lives far away, and I haven't thought of her for years. Where did her memory come from?

Oh boy, I sure messed up _____, what am I to do? I can fixate on making a mistake for a while.

We need purified water for the humidifier. I think this thought as I am driving away from the store and wish I would have remembered sooner.

You are likely thinking, why didn't Heather make a list? I do, and did, and it is on the app on my phone, but I don't always look at it, believing I can do it on my own. Hahahaha, that is so not true.

By reviewing what happens when my brain is under the driving influence, I realize ideas definitely do pop into my head (and the list seems endless). But I still want to think I create my thoughts. More research on my part is needed for me to believe I don't. Stubborn you say? Yes, a wee bit.

WE STORE WHAT WORKS

What I do know is, as we go about our day, our mind is constantly having to assess what we know, what we need to know, and must decide what to do next. We are forever dealing with change, adjustment, and the need to be flexible. As we move through our life with things constantly changing, experience is one of our greatest teachers because we store what has worked in the past to use in the future. The past is not only what we personally experienced and learned, it is also that of our predecessors who passed down old DNA and the instincts they developed.

Our ancestor's DNA not only determines characteristics like being shy or outgoing, blue eyes or brown, curly hair or straight, but also our mindset and thought process. Their old DNA lives on in each of us, and the associated instincts and our needs are the result of all the experiences they had. When we analyze our predecessors, it is easy to understand many of our fears and worries.

The ancient inherited qualities we have been dealt create obstacles to getting a grip because they influence us to think thoughts which are negative, cause us to worry, fill us with fear, and ensure we judge each and every person we meet. I developed a theory about the role this old DNA plays in our present-day way of thinking. There is no scientific proof to my theory, but I am convinced this makes a lot of sense as to why we do what we do and think what we think. Let me explain this theory of mine.

We are descendants of those who survived in times of trouble, disease, development, migration, and lots of change, etc. Not only that, but they were the ones who produced offspring, lucky us, to carry on their legacy. Our ancestors had to have the ability to sense danger, so they were forever looking at life through a negative lens and judging people and situations. Because our ancestors were the ones who survived, it is obvious they learned to be prepared for the worst or they learned to quickly respond to surprises when they were caught off guard. This meant they were always thinking about how things could go wrong rather than how things are right, because survival demanded this of them. They were always on edge; convinced disaster was imminent. This instinct, passed on to us, makes us sense doom and gloom at every turn, puts us on the defense, and ensures we tend to view life and people through a negative lens.

Another influence on our thinking comes from the fact that our predecessors survived in large part because they gathered in groups of people who were worthy of their trust. It was vital that they lived in a community of like-minded people who worked well as a team, protected each other, and could fight off intruders, both human and animal. All community members needed to hunt and gather food for the group. They had to obey communal rules and be loyal to each other. They learned to judge and test people for how strong, smart, and quick they were; it was important that members of the group were mighty and agile.

Fast forward to now and think about how we like to join groups of like-minded people. We come together over a favorite sports team, political alliance, religious affiliation, etc. When we look back at our history it makes sense that we like to be tribal, because having our group means we will have a better chance of survival. When you transfer this knowledge of our ancestors to the importance we place on friendships, you realize we can't have it any other way. We all talk about our social circles, who we know, and what groups we belong to. Our need for our group started when we were young. We struggled with our desire for a "bestie and didn't understand then that friendships would change many times. As a young child we had no idea a best friend would take years to develop, we just had an insatiable need for one special person in our life. Maybe even continuing this need to today. More on this in chapter XX.

INSTINCTS PASSED DOWN TO US

Old DNA influences on our thoughts make certain we constantly notice, watch, worry, analyze, and feel on edge. Even though today very little danger lurks in the shadows of our lives, our mind is certain there is something amiss, so it is no surprise that everyone talks about feeling stressed. But the stress we feel is mostly self-inflicted. We no longer need to hunt and gather because we can shop at any number of grocery stores where food of all kinds, in all seasons, is available to us. Even so, we still have stocked pantry shelves and freezers filled with non-essential food, just in case.

We continue to have the urge to judge situations as safe and others on their ability to be worthy. We judge people as weak or strong, athletic or wimpy. We are forever on the lookout for smart, quick-witted friends who are confident and slightly arrogant, certain these are the qualities of survival success. We look for besties who can be trusted with our secrets and desires. We want to have a social group to which we belong and are convinced it is vital that we are considered socially acceptable, and fit in. All of these thoughts weigh us down.

WE LEARN ALL SORTS OF THINGS

Our thoughts are not only influenced by the past, old DNA, experience, and instincts, but also by the people we live with and learn from. As children and parents, we all experience "on the job training".

While growing up, we learn how the world works, who people are, and how we should act. We develop our sense of self from the experiences and people we encounter. And as parents, we tend to pass along the same things we learned as kids to our own children.

The things we learn as a child may seem simple on the surface - what specific colors are, the smell of baked cookies (or cake, bread, etc.), the sound of music (different instruments make different sounds), the feeling of hunger (and what to do about it), the sound of anger, the feeling of love – but they are actually complicated. As a child, we learn intricate ideas with many layers, and if learned without specific instruction, we create reasons and stories to explain how and why they are the way they are even though what we come up with isn't true. Nor do our thoughts make sense.

Children are too young to question what they see, and they are taught that authority figures must be believed at all costs. So now, as a "grown-up", it is very important that we carefully scrutinize what we gleaned from childhood and carried through life. Part of getting a grip involves learning which thoughts and beliefs are accurate. The good news is that not all of what we learned when we were young is wrong or bad.

SOME BELIEFS ARE GOOD

Plenty of the people in my life have had a positive influence on my thinking and taught me things from which I learned valuable lessons. My father taught me to always take my own wheels so I can leave when I want or need to. My husband taught me to "make it a great day" rather than to wait to have one, and a childhood friend inspires me daily on social media to make happy happen.

One of the best mantras I ever learned helps me push myself, and it especially did just that while I was living in Austria. I was not overcome with fear after that day I told you about because I believe everyone must take advantage of opportunities, even when they are uncomfortable. My mantra, "Take advantage of every opportunity that comes your way" came from my mother's cousin John, in Scotland, whom I met when I was 17.

Cousin John was a character to say the very least. I could tell you one tale after another because I enjoyed him that much. In the few short days I spent with him and his family, he taught me a lot about living life fully. He opened my eyes to having an opinion and taught me that stating it doesn't have to be considered rude. My epiphany about opportunity happened while watching him interact with his children, dressed in their school uniforms ready to go for the day, lined up at the front door, waiting for him to impart his words of wisdom. That morning he was telling them not to talk about the hunting outing he and his friends had the day before during which some bird shot ended up in someone's backside (that wasn't supposed to happen). He told his children specifically to not talk about what had happened, gossiping is unbecoming (duly noted and something I too believe). He finished talking to them by saying "Take advantage of every opportunity that comes your way."

Those words rocked my young world and I snagged them as my own. I believe they are true genius and I use them to this day. And just like my saying, GET A GRIP, his words have spurred me on when I needed it and pushed me to try things I didn't think I could do.

SOME BELIEFS ARE NOT GOOD

Other people influenced me in the opposite way, and I have worked hard to overcome the thoughts and beliefs they instilled. Somehow, and somewhere along my journey I learned to believe friends would leave me and they were not to be trusted. I didn't know this was deeply embedded in my brain until much later in life. And when I heard this thought, I was shocked. Where on earth did that belief come from? I could never figure that out, but once I caught myself thinking this thought I understood that was what was holding me back from making close friends, so I worked to change it.

As a young child an authority figure taught me about standing tall and walking gracefully. Without explanation, and me being too young to question, I decided this meant if you stood and walked properly you were the best type of human. As I grew up, I noticed plenty of not-so-great people stand tall and walk gracefully. Once I started to analyze my childhood belief, I realized my thoughts weren't true. I now know the intended message was to stand tall and walk gracefully because people assess you as confident and capable and consequently take you seriously, but without the proper explanation, and because I was young when I developed my belief, I made up my own reason, which was false.

In my youth I was taught to obey authority figures and that they were totally in charge. When I was in school, if any of the students did something wrong in class, like talking to a neighbor, the teacher put that student at the front of the room with their back to the class and their nose pushed into a circle drawn on the board. The intent was to shame the child for stepping outside the rules. Those days left an indelible mark on all of us, but especially me because I regularly liked to talk to my neighbor. The received message was we had to act a certain way to be worthy, and we all took that message to heart. You too may have had such experiences and your children might be experiencing them right now.

As a young person, did you ever hear an authority figure say:

- Why can't you make your bed?
- Stop crying like a baby.
- Why can't you be like your sister (brother)?
- Sit still!
- I didn't receive your homework, again.
- Why are you always late?

Or maybe you saw them roll their eyes when you made a misstep, or sigh when it took you time to do something, and as a result, you developed the belief that you must act in a certain way to be acceptable and loved which then transferred to a fear of doing something wrong that would make others not like you.

Children start life with rose-colored glasses that allow them to see the beauty in everything, but it doesn't take long for them to learn to think otherwise.

We all started out believing in ourselves and our abilities completely, even beyond reason. If you ask a group of first graders who can play the piano, most will raise their hands, shaking them wildly with such enthusiasm that you believe they are concert virtuosi even though they aren't even sure what a piano is or what it means to be able to play one.

Sadly, as they age, they become ruled by critical thoughts and controlled by the emotions that come from their negative view of who they are and what they can do. Don't believe me? Ask a group of talented adult piano players who can play the piano well and very few wildly shake their raised hand.

Over my years in education, I have watched happy go lucky, curious, into everything toddlers turn into children who question themselves, feel insecure, and worry they aren't enough.

By high school, these same kids are totally flooded with thoughts of:

I'm not -----

  · as good as the other students in my class
  · smart enough
  · good looking enough
  · talented enough

They are afraid of what the future holds and they believe the glass is half-empty, things are scarce, people are bad, and times are hard. And as they turn into adults, just like us, they continue on with these fears and worries.

OUR SENSE OF SELF

Not only do we think thoughts about how harsh the world is, our self-image is based on underdeveloped, unexplained, not well thought out assumptions we developed as children. When we get right down to it and remember how we were treated when we were young by the authority figures around us, it is easy to understand that our self-image is centered on being worthy.

The negative view of who we are was influenced by the words we heard, and the actions we saw, especially from the people who had authority over us. This image is reinforced today as we move through our fast paced, social media driven, I am cooler than you are modern times.

Our unworthy self-image is reinforced by the pesky inherited old DNA which considers "worthy" important, because when we are worthy, we are acceptable as a member of a group and that means we have a better chance of survival. Do we still need to worry about this? No, but without some work on our part to change, we do worry. As you learn and implement the strategies I present to you, which are necessary to GET A GRIP, you can overcome the worry about being worthy by gaining a better sense of who you really are; unique and necessary.

Most of us have an unworthy view of ourselves and it comes up at the strangest times. When we do things for others, even when we don't want to, when we try to be the life of the party, even though we are feeling down, or when we want to be the most popular in the group, these are the times that we need to realize we are trying to prove our worthiness.

As young people, we were very susceptible to becoming overwhelmed by our thoughts and emotions, especially when thinking about our worthiness or lack thereof. Instead of focusing on what is good about ourselves, we created a self-image based on what we believed is wrong with us. We made up stories in our mind about what others think, and ended up filling our heads with fear, worry and judgment. Today, with all the added pressures of social media, the level of anxiety and depression in people has gone through the roof. Worst of all, suicide is now a constant threat.

Since we learned to be wary and judgmental from eons of practice, our heads are filled with anxious thoughts and depression is often present in our worried mind. We focus on our problems to keep our mind occupied, but most of these problems are just figments of our imagination. This type of thinking pattern develops early, but parents and teachers only start to notice it in children around grade four. It is at this age that children start to think big adult thoughts because old DNA is activated by having to take care of oneself. Life demands survival, and being independent means children take the helm and when they do, they imagine all that can go wrong so they will be prepared. Adults continue this thought process and convince themselves that something is amiss.

OUR THOUGHTS CENTER ON PROBLEMS

When I see an accomplished, put together, "on top of their game" person, only to learn they struggle with their emotions, I am reminded that we create drama and angst for ourselves just by what we think. It is as if everyone wants to believe they are not good enough, life is awful, and no one is nice. We have done this for so long we have developed a bad habit of thinking negative thoughts.

Because our inherited brain likes to be on high alert, we think being busy, especially mentally, is important, and even though life is grand we invent problems to work on. For example, as you wake in the morning, warm in your bed after a good night's sleep, with everything in your life in order, your brain still creates thoughts that something is wrong. As we go about our day, we continue this trend and worry about anything to keep busy, even if it is something as trivial as whether the toilet paper should roll over or under, or the seat/lid should be up or down. (Trust me, I know that it should roll over and be down).

As if this wasn't enough, we are driven to believe what we think is true. This is the biggest trap of all. Just because we think it doesn't make it true. It's actually just a thought.

Life isn't awful, and things aren't worse today than in the past, although that is exactly what most people think. Look at history, things have gone well more than they haven't because we are here, and we are successful as a human race even though we are convinced it is otherwise.

WE ARE BORN WITH PROMISE AND POTENTIAL

To change this negative self-image and downtrodden view of the world, every time these thoughts pop up, and in order to think in the GET A GRIP way, you must understand you were born a special gem, full of promise and potential, we all were. I have always believed one of the greatest things in life is you, frankly, each and every one of us. Don't believe me? Well, it is true. Everywhere on earth, all the people here, and yes you too, were born a unique element and were put here to be part of life's chemistry to do the things only they can do. Yet, the experiences of life talked each of us out of believing we are an essential element in our humanity compound, and we have forgotten how to love ourselves.

To GET A GRIP, it is mandatory that we learn to take control of our thoughts so we can create the feelings and actions that fulfill our promise and potential. It will take some work, but you can learn to love yourself and stop the negative mind banter that lives in your head. That is exactly what I teach you how to do in the following pages.

In addition to loving yourself again, like you did when you were a child with rose colored glasses, a return to happiness will be your big reward when you learn to GET A GRIP, because happy isn't something that just happens to you, it is something you work to gain by controlling your thoughts.

To fully change what we think, feel, and do, and in order to reach our promise and potential, let's learn how to GET A GRIP!

V. CHANGING A HABIT

The patterns of our lives reveal us. Our habits measure us.
Mary Oliver

Before we get into the specifics of learning to get a grip, it is important that we know how it will feel and what it will require. To make the most of life and reach our promise and potential we must GET A GRIP and to GET A GRIP we first need to change our habits of thought. When I say habits, most people think of those pesky things we do that we don't know we are doing, yet when we take note, wish we wouldn't. That perfectly describes the habits of thought that stand in our way of getting a grip.

CHANGING A HABIT REQUIRES EFFORT

Habits are the things we do automatically without having to think. Some habits are good. We need them. Our brain needs us to develop habits because doing things on autopilot conserves energy. It is good for us to develop the habit of brushing our teeth, exercising, going to bed at a certain time, etc. But other habits we developed are not good for us, like overeating, being judgmental, procrastinating, overspending, biting our nails, or being glued to our phones.

All habits, whether good or bad, create pathways in our brains, known scientifically as neural pathways. I picture these pathways as roads and intersections in our brains. When we create a habit by doing something repeatedly, good or bad, our electrical impulses (neurons) run down the roads, go through intersections, continue on to their destination, and form deep grooves. Because of the saying "you are in a rut", I imagine these deep grooves as ruts in a mud road which have dried and hardened. If you have ever driven on such a road, you know all too well how hard it is to get out of a rut. In the same way, it is equally hard when trying to make a change to any habit. If you brush your teeth in the morning, try not doing that and you will realize even changing a good habit can feel terrible.

As we are trying to reach our goal of getting a grip and making changes to our thought habits, we must get out of the deeply grooved neural pathway to develop a new, better way of thinking. We don't want to change our good habits, just the bad ones, most especially those that aren't helping us GET A GRIP.

CHANGE FEELS WEIRD AND AWKWARD

Making these changes will feel weird and awkward in the beginning. To illustrate how awful change feels, I want you to cross your arms like your mother or father did when she/he was disappointed with you. Now look down and see if you put right over left or left over right. Whichever you did, I want you to now do the opposite. Did you notice it isn't easy to do and that you actually have to think hard to complete that task? Did you notice it felt awkward and you wanted to put it back to the way it "should be"? That is how it will feel as you start to make the changes necessary to GET A GRIP. But do it anyway.

Even though it will feel awkward and weird, thankfully new pathways are easy to make. As you persist to think in a different way and do it repeatedly, after a while your newly created habits of thought will be strengthened. They will take less effort and will become your new normal. A good example of this is if you continue to cross your arms in the opposite way to what you normally do, and do it consistently every time for long enough, it will feel natural.

Old DNA and inherited thought processes make sure our brain will fight change with all its might, so altering the way we think requires motivation which, as we all know, ebbs and flows.

SYSTEMS, ROUTINES, AND SMALL FIRST STEPS

There are some tricks of the trade when it comes to changing a habit, staying motivated, and reaching our goals. Research on change says to be successful we must set up systems, follow routines, and trick ourselves with small first steps. Let me explain each of these elements.

Systems are how things influence one another when talking about the entire idea. Many elements work together to make us healthy and able to GET A GRIP. We can use this knowledge to create systems that help us do what it takes to change our habits of thought.

One of the best systems I have ever used is to receive a reminder for my goals. For example, my digital calendar reminds me each morning it's time to go to the gym.

When I am trying to remember anything, but especially when I am trying to break a habit, I like to be reminded, and often. Back in the day, before I had a smartphone that buzzes reminders, or before watches that do the same thing, I used post it notes everywhere to try to remember everything I had to do. Imagine little yellow squares on my car windows impeding my vision and when I would roll down the window, out they would fly, along with my memory. As you can imagine, it didn't work very well.

Searching for a successful system, I changed my approach and decided to staple a folded note to my jacket or blouse. (Surprisingly, the staples never damaged any of my clothing). It worked for me because during the day people pointed to the note

I'd forgotten was there and asked me what it was. I would look down to where they had pointed and respond with a touch of surprise, "Oh, that is something I need to remember." And because they asked, I not only remembered the note was stapled to my shirt, but also what the note said. This was my technology free, several-a-day reminders, all solicited from other people.

Thankfully, I was able to transition to two far more useful systems. One of them I use is a dry erase marker to write reminders on my bathroom mirror, so I see them during my morning and nightly routines. If I wake during the night, I also write what thoughts I need to remember on the same mirror. The second is my smartphone coupled with my digital calendar which sends me reminders throughout the day. I can now rely on these systems to be on top of my game without the help of people questioning my fashion sense.

Take exercise as another example. Perhaps you want to get in shape and plan to work out for an hour each day. This idea guarantees immediate and total failure. First, because carving out an hour in your day, right out of the gate, is overwhelming to even think about. And working out for an hour may just make you so sore you will never again want to exercise, ever.

But if I told you to start with five minutes of gentle stretching Monday through Friday you would likely say "you bet." Five minutes of gentle stretching is a great way to start an exercise habit. To get the recommended 10,000 steps a day seems daunting until you break it down and start with 500 and add increments of 100. We don't need to be all the way to the final goal at the beginning. We can gently work our way there.

Routines also help us go about our day. Most of us do certain things in a certain way each morning to get ready. Maybe you, like some, immediately make your bed. That one takes some time for me, but I do it before long. Most people I know who work, shower in the morning to help them wake up. Your routine might look something like this. Alarm goes off, you hit the snooze once or twice, then you finally rise and stumble into the bathroom. You likely "use the facilities", further shuffle into the kitchen to make coffee, go back to the bathroom to brush your teeth, shave if you need to, shower, go get the now made coffee, dress, do your hair, and finally go to eat some breakfast.

To change a habit, we can use our already set routines and insert bits and pieces that help us complete our goals to GET A GRIP.

Small first steps are how we can trick ourselves into doing what needs to be done to change our habits. And by starting with a tiny change, aligned with our daily routines which are part of a system we create, these small first steps help us stay on track and motivated to make the changes we set for ourselves.

VI.   TRACKING YOUR PROGRESS

*Excellence, then, being of these two kinds,
intellectual and moral, intellectual excellence
owes its birth and growth mainly to instruction,
and so requires time and experience, while
moral excellence is the result of habit or custom.*
Aristotle

Changing thinking habits requires keeping a record of progress. Why? Because when you document and see you have done something for several days in a row, you will want to maintain the streak. And maintaining a streak means you will accomplish your goal.

CREATE A SYSTEM OF RECORD KEEPING

I am a math person and therefore I adore keeping track of evidence and using spreadsheets to look for patterns and predict outcomes. As a teacher we are often asked to take on other classes and while I was teaching a class on health and wellness to sixth and seventh graders, I happened upon one form of record keeping that rocked my view of changing a habit. I read a description of how Benjamin Franklin went about setting personal goals and the system of record keeping he used to achieve them.

In his autobiography, Mr. Franklin describes 13 virtues he chose for himself to improve. I thought his choices were interesting and so I am including them for you to see. I find it important to note that over the course of history humans have been doing the same things. His list with definitions is as follows:

Temperance. Eat not to dullness; drink not to elevation.

Silence. Speak not but what may benefit others or yourself; avoid trifling conversation.

Order. Let all your things have their places; let each part of your business have its time.

Resolution. Resolve to perform what you ought; perform without fail what you resolve.

Frugality. Make no expense but to do good to others or yourself; i.e., waste nothing.

Industry. Lose no time; be always busy in something useful; cut off all unnecessary actions.

Sincerity. Use no hurtful deceit; think innocently and justly, and, if you speak, speak accordingly.

Justice. Wrong none by doing injuries or omitting the benefits that are your duty.

Moderation. Avoid extremes; forbear resenting injuries so much as you think they deserve.

Cleanliness. Tolerate no uncleanliness in body, clothes, or habitation.

Tranquility. Be not disturbed at trifles, or at accidents common or unavoidable.

Chastity. Rarely use venery but for health or offspring, never to dullness, weakness, or the injury of your own or another's peace or reputation.

Humility. Imitate Jesus and Socrates.

Benjamin Franklin decided the best way to work on each habit was one at a time. He realized that one virtue leads to another, so he arranged them in the order they were to be mastered, as in the list above.

He worked on one virtue per week. To record his progress, he made a little book that contained one page for each of the 13 virtues.

FORM OF THE PAGES.

TEMPERANCE.

Eat not to dulness: drink not to elevation.

	Sun.	M.	T.	W.	Th.	F.	S.
Tem.							
Sil.	*	*		*		*	
Ord.	*	*	*		*	*	*
Res.		*				*	
Fru.		*				*	
Ind.			*				
Sinc.							
Jus.							
Mod.							
Clea.							
Tran.							
Chas.							
Hum.							

Take temperance for example. During each day of the week, if he wasn't temperate, he would place a little black mark on that day. And because he was focused on this virtue, it isn't a stretch of the imagination to think there wouldn't be any marks for temperance.

Even though he wasn't focused on the other virtues he would mark on the day they happened.

The second week he worked on Silence, and because he had already strengthened temperance, it made sense that both top lines were blank. It might not work out that way, but hopefully it did. He completed 13 weeks to finish one round of virtues and he repeated it four times in the first year. The second year he went through the 13-week exercise just once. And after that he completed one every several years and then eventually none at all.

We can use a similar plan for changing thought habits which are obstacles to getting a grip. We will need to do this every day, every month, and repeat it as long as it takes to GET A GRIP. When we have learned a better mindset, we can continue as needed.

SCHEDULE

Our "virtues" will be the thought strategies I teach you in this book. I believe working on one per week, and one at a time in the order I created, is a great way to GET A GRIP. I know life is busy so I also offer a six-week schedule. I ordered our "virtues" in such a way so that by the time we are doing the heavy lifting of changing what triggers us we will be ready to tackle that challenge. And I placed mind mapping at the end because it requires all the other skills to be able to do it.

Instead of noticing all of them as Mr. Franklin did, you have two choices.

One - work on one thing each week for thirteen weeks. I created checklists and journal pages which you can use immediately. I include more in-depth worksheets if you are so inclined. No matter which, track your accomplishments.

Or two - work on combined topics for a six-week program. I include this schedule along with journal pages in chapter XXII.

Now for the learning.

VII.   OVERCOME OBSTACLES TO GET A GRIP

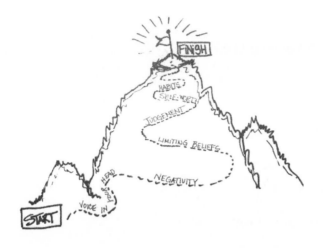

Happiness doesn't start with a relationship, a vacation, a job, or money. It starts with you thinking and what you tell yourself every day.
Fabio Trabison @The_positivequote

The way we think dictates how we feel, and although everyone thinks in their own way, there are a few common roadblocks to getting and maintaining our grip on life. Each of these roadblocks is no more than a thinking habit, and you and I both know habits, when they are bad, need to be broken.

I have chosen the following roadblocks for you to work on because in my experience these are what we all struggle with and are the thinking obstacles that cause us the most mental grief.

THINKING OBSTACLES

Our obstacles are thinking judgmental thoughts, negative thinking, fear, worry, hearing your self-talk in your head, limiting beliefs, triggers and setting relationship boundaries.

The list of skills you will be working on:

Gratitude Journaling

1. Catch Yourself Thinking

2. The Voice in Our Head

3. Is that true?

4. Negative Repetitive Thinking

5. Limiting Beliefs

6. Fear - Is it fear or excitement?

7. Worry - And Then What?

8. Judging Others/Ourselves

9. Am I ...?

10. Triggers - Breathe

11. Plan Ahead

12. Circle of Trust

13. Mind Mapping

If you choose the 13-week schedule you will work on each of these in the list for one week.

However, if you choose the six-week schedule you will combine the topics as follows:

Week One- Gratitude Journaling, Catch Yourself Thinking, Hearing the self-talk in your head, Is What I Am Thinking True?

Week Two - Negative Repetitive Thinking, Limiting Beliefs

Week Three - Fear, Worry, And Then What?

Week Four - Judging - Ourselves and others, Am I?

Week Five - Triggers, Planning Ahead, Circle of Trust

Week Six - Mind Mapping

And while working on each topic you can choose the simple tracking progress or choose the more in-depth tracking. I suggest you choose the simple one when what you are learning is something you already do, and choose the more in-depth record keeping when you are needing more help with a topic.

I included different tracking sheets at the end of each chapter. Choose either six weeks or thirteen and use the sheets to track your progress and to list your gratitudes and joy. The journal pages and tracking pages are for you to use but you can also create your own.

There is also a separate Journal to purchase if you would like the tracking and journaling all in one place.

So, let's start at the beginning of the work necessary to GET A GRIP.

VIII. START YOUR DAY RIGHT

We are what we repeatedly do. Excellence,
therefore, is not an act, but a habit.
Will Durant

To Get A Grip we will have to change our thinking habits, and this is hard, and demands that we do what needs to be done, when it needs to be done, whether we want to or not.

MAKE YOUR BED

One way to train ourselves to accomplish tasks even when we don't want to, is to do things a certain way, at a certain time, every time. One of my favorite order activities I do for myself, and what I recommend to you too, actually anyone who is willing to listen, is to make the bed first thing in the morning. Not only make the bed, but do it well, with the sheets smooth, the covers pulled flat and the pillows fluffed and placed in their appropriate spots. And if it doesn't work first thing in the morning (maybe because there is someone still in the bed as you head off for your day) do it at some time before you retire in the evening. A study of millionaires noted that over 80% made their bed each day. Why? It instills the ability to make yourself complete tasks you may not want to do, which helps you demand your best.

GRATITUDE JOURNALING

Morning is the perfect time to set the tone for your day and work on thinking thoughts that are accurate and helpful. Nighttime routines also play a large role in how our days play out.

Start each day with a routine that orders your day in the way you desire. I start my day while still in bed. I call this routine Peeling off Negative Nancy. (Let me apologize to anyone named Nancy who is reading this. I only use your name because it sounds good with negative, and I don't think anyone who is named Nancy is negative, so please forgive the reference.) Because of my predisposed anxious mind, I tend to think thoughts that are negative. Knowing this, I Peel Off Negative Nancy before getting out of bed by stating all the wonderful things in my life for which I am grateful. I do this so I can recenter my thoughts on the wonderful aspects of my life, rather than auguring in on what I make believe is wrong. You too can start your day with Peeling off Negative Nancy.

To do this you will start each day with Gratitude. As you wake, while still in your bed, think of things for which you are grateful. Then, while prepping in the mirror, or brushing your teeth, think of more. After you are dressed, think of even more.

You may find several wonderful things in your life are hard to think of at first, and they are, but as you do this each day, you will realize it gets easier. Each day say different things so that you stretch your list about what is right with your world.

To begin this habit, you will do this physically by writing in a journal, but as you get going you can do this in your head or better yet on your phone. Choose a journal to keep track of your gratitudes, start small and write one to five things in the morning that you are grateful for.

You can do this with your loved ones too and teach them this valuable skill. At breakfast, take a moment together to talk through the things for which they are grateful.

At night, as you get ready for bed, you are to note what brought you joy during your day. Even if your day wasn't fantastic, look for small things that were good. Write these in your journal.

TRACKING YOUR PROGRESS

Gratitude journaling and recording joy will be done every day, every week. At the top of each recording page, just like the one shown below, you will see a spot to place your dot for Gratitude Journaling. There should be two dots per day to note morning gratitude and night joys.

EVERY DAY
Tracking Progress

GRATITUDE /JOY JOURNAL							
MAKE YOUR BED EVERY DAY START AND END YOUR DAY WITH NOTES ON HOW FORTUNATE YOUR ARE							
	SUN	MON	TUES	WED	THUR	FRI	SAT
MAKE YOUR BED							
GRATITUDE JOURNAL							

These are included on every tracking sheet because they are to be done every day.

Morning - make my bed and write down things for which I am grateful

Evening – record what brought you joy today

IX. WEEK ONE – CATCH YOURSELF THINKING

There is nothing either good or bad
but thinking makes it so.
William Shakespeare

The first big step toward GET A GRIP is to notice your thoughts and hear the useless noise in your thinking. I call this catching yourself thinking because at first you will not realize you are thinking. But as you focus your attention, you will learn to catch your thoughts as they happen. Learning to catch your thoughts takes a bit of practice and starts with noticing that you are thinking.

Here is a personal example.

When I was young, I was enthralled with the TV show Bewitched. In that series, Samantha, the central figure in the show, was a quintessential sixties housewife who, unbeknownst to her husband and most everyone, was actually a witch. To work her magic, she twitched her nose. Well, you can imagine, as an impressionable child who loved make believe, I picked up making a funny movement with my mouth and face to make my nose move, not exactly like hers, but I still thought it was super cool. This practiced twitch of mine became a habit. It looked strange, and it developed into a tick I didn't even notice I was doing. In an effort to get me to stop, when my mother saw me do it, she would say, as only a mother can, STOP THAT. Each time she did I flinched, and realized I was doing the nose twitch thing again. I did want to stop, especially before the movement ruined the cartilage in my nose as she suggested it would. It took time and lots of effort, but as I focused my attention, I finally caught myself contorting my face, and I grabbed my nose. At that moment I was able to stop completely because I finally caught myself.

In the same way, you must catch yourself thinking before you can start to rework your thoughts and GET A GRIP. As you catch your thoughts, you might wonder about their origin. I know I did.

WHAT IF

Many years ago, as I started my journey of improving my thinking, I didn't understand much about mindset and I grabbed onto any idea or tip that sounded like it might help and clung to it for dear life. The first "grab" I made came from the Midwest Center for Anxiety created by Lucinda Bassett. I learned about "what if" thinking from her. Before studying her work, I had no idea that because of my predisposed anxiety I like to be prepared for the worst thing that could possibly happen, and endlessly allowed myself to ponder, what if?

What if thinking can be thoughts like:

> What if I faint?

> What if I get in a wreck and die?

What if I get sick?

What if I say something stupid at the party tonight?

What if I get fired?

Because of this endless banter I was worn out after each episode of what if thinking. Talk about noise in my head, right?

At that early stage in my learning about mindset I was trying to understand why I worried so much and, because of Lucinda Bassett, I had a good start. If you worry a lot, you likely think in a similar way. As you catch yourself thinking, you might find that many of your thoughts are centered on prepping for the worst. Lucinda taught me that what if thinking is typical for people with anxiety. Once I knew what to watch for, I was able to catch myself thinking what if and stop. Just noticing your thoughts is the first step to GET A GRIP. It doesn't matter what you are thinking, just that you notice you are doing so.

Catch yourself thinking is the first obstacle to work on because without noticing what and how you are thinking, you don't stand a chance of changing your ingrained habit of thinking, which runs on autopilot.

For this first step, I suggest you start simply and check your thoughts a few times throughout the day. Because this is something new, it helps to set an alarm on your phone or smart watch to remind you to stop and listen to what you are thinking. Each time a reminder buzzes, check your thoughts. Notice what type of thoughts you are thinking. Are they centered on what if? Or are they judgmental, negative, fear based, or all about worry? With practice you will start to check in with your thoughts on your own, without a reminder, but in the beginning, you will need an external mother's voice saying STOP THAT.

Create a System - Decide what times work easily for you to check in with your thoughts. Once times are set, schedule those "appointments" on a digital calendar. Then, repeat these appointments for several days until you become accustomed to catching yourself thinking throughout the day. The glory of these reminders is that when it is time to check in with your thoughts you will get a notification to stop for a few minutes and check in with your brain.

Routine – Make the habit of catching yourself thinking easy by imbedding check-in times into your already set routines. What works best is to choose times that are already part of your day like

- when you are brushing your teeth in the morning

- while at work during scheduled breaks

- or when you take a bathroom break

For me, I can input catching myself thinking into my desire to walk a minimum of 250 steps per hour. A buzzer reminds me to move at 10 minutes to the hour. And when it does, I not only get up and move, but I also concentrate on where my mind is wandering.

Small first step – Choose just one "appointment" time to start with, do that for a few days, and then work up from there to several times per day.

CALENDAR WITH REMINDERS

Set up a digital calendar, if you can, that works with all your devices. Input reminders for the goals you set. Use this digital calendar to also help organize your life by inputting appointments, scheduled weekly engagements, and random required details of your days, weeks, and months.

Digital calendars are great to use because you can set yearly reminders. We all know booking dental appointments, yearly doctor visits, wellness checkups, smoke alarm battery changes, and so many other details can derail us if we forget them.

One of my favorite uses of a digital calendar is to remind me of upcoming birthdays so I can remember to reach out and send an electronic birthday card, I never seem to remember in time for sending one via post.

If you don't have access to a digital calendar then make use of your journal and keep track of daily reminders there.

TRACKING PROGRESS - WEEK ONE

CATCH YOURSELF THINKING							
THROUGHOUT YOUR DAY, TAKE TIME TO NOTICE WHAT YOU ARE THINKING							
	SUN	MON	TUES	WED	THUR	FRI	SAT
MAKE YOUR BED							
GRATITUDE/JOY JOURNAL							
CATCH YOURSELF THINKING							

Sunday – In contrast to what so many believe, our old DNA brain runs one task at a time and does not multitask. As you focus on your thoughts, only work on catching yourself thinking. Ignore all other distractions.

Monday – Take responsibility for your thinking. As you focus on catching yourself thinking, avoid judgement of your thoughts.

Tuesday – As you notice your thoughts, write notes on the type of thoughts you are thinking. Are they worries, fears, judgments? Are they negative? Create a labeling system for the type of thoughts you think, and after several days of recording, look for patterns.

Wednesday – As you notice your thoughts today, are they productive? Or just noise?

Thursday – As you gain confidence catching your thinking, you can start to analyze if what you tend to think is true. Are you holding onto your beliefs with a death grip? Could you loosen your grasp and change your thought patterns to truly GET A GRIP?

Friday – Do you tend to notice the good things that happen to you or more so the bad?

Saturday – Do you focus your thoughts on what you want? Or on what you don't want?

JOURNAL PAGE
13 WEEK SCHEDULE - WEEK ONE

CATCH YOURSELF THINKING							
THROUGHOUT YOUR DAY, TAKE TIME TO NOTICE WHAT YOU ARE THINKING							
	SUN	MON	TUES	WED	THUR	FRI	SAT
MAKE YOUR BED							
GRATITUDE/JOY JOURNAL							
CATCH YOURSELF THINKING							

GRATITUDES   JOY   GRATITUDES   JOY
MONDAY   **FRIDAY**
1.   1.   1.   1.
2.   2.   2.   2.
3.   3.   3.   3.
4.   4.   4.   4.
5.   5.   5.   5.

TUESDAY   **SATURDAY**
1.   1.   1.   1.
2.   2.   2.   2.
3.   3.   3.   3.
4.   4.   4.   4.
5.   5.   5.   5.

WEDNESDAY   **SUNDAY**
1.   1.   1.   1.
2.   2.   2.   2.
3.   3.   3.   3.
4.   4.   4.   4.
5.   5.   5.   5.

THURSDAY
1.   1.
2.   2.
3.   3.
4.   4.
5.   5.

MORE IN DEPTH TRACKING
SUNDAY THROUGH SATURDAY

CATCH YOURSELF THINKING							
THROUGHOUT YOUR DAY, TAKE TIME TO NOTICE WHAT YOU ARE THINKING							
	SUN	MON	TUES	WED	THUR	FRI	SAT
MAKE YOUR BED							
GRATITUDE/JOY JOURNAL							
CATCH YOURSELF THINKING							

Continue to make your bed and journal each morning and night. Add your notes each day on what you catch yourself thinking.

Sunday

Our old DNA brain runs one task at a time and does not multitask. As you focus on your thoughts, only work on catching yourself thinking. Ignore all other distractions.

TIME OF DAY	WHAT WERE YOU THINKING?

Monday

Take responsibility for your thinking. As you focus on catching yourself thinking, avoid judgement of your thoughts.

TIME OF DAY	WHAT WERE YOU THINKING?

Tuesday

Are your thoughts, worries, fears, judgments? Are they negative? Create a labeling system for the type of thoughts you think and look for patterns.

TIME OF DAY	WHAT WERE YOU THINKING?	TYPE OF THOUGHT

Wednesday

Today are your thoughts productive? Or just noise?

TIME	WHAT WERE YOU THINKING?	PRODUCTIVE OR NOISE

Thursday

Analyze if what you tend to think is true. Are you holding onto your beliefs with a death grip? Could you loosen your grasp and change your thought patterns to truly GET A GRIP?

TIME	WHAT WERE YOU THINKING?	TRUE OR FALSE

Friday

Do you tend to notice the good things that happen to you or the bad?

TIME	WHAT WERE YOU THINKING?	GOOD OR BAD

Saturday

Do you focus your thoughts on what you want? Or on what you don't want? On what you want to have happen or what you want to avoid?

TIMES	WHAT WERE YOU THINKING?	WANT OR AVOID?

X. WEEK TWO - SELF TALK

Watch your thoughts, they become words;
watch your words, they become actions;
watch your actions, they become habits;
watch your habits, they become character;
watch your character, for it becomes your destiny.
Frank Outlaw

Your random, vague, unrealistic thoughts come from mind messages silently playing in the background of your brain generated by what is known as "the voice in your head" or otherwise known as self-talk.

THE WAY WE TALK TO OURSELVES

As you gain skill in catching yourself thinking, and hearing your thoughts, you will notice that you say disparaging comments in your head. When you make a mistake or do what you deem is the wrong thing, have you ever silently told yourself how dumb you are? When you wake up late and are in a rush, do you berate yourself for sleeping in? I told you about old DNA and thus you can understand why you judge yourself harshly, all because you need to be ready for anything and everything, right? But is that working in your favor today? Is it helping you to GET A GRIP? I think we can all agree that when we talk trash about ourselves, it doesn't work out for the best. Overcoming this obstacle is a big step on the path to GET A GRIP and relies on controlling the voice in your head.

Who is the voice in your head, you ask? An all-time favorite book for me is "The New Earth" by Eckhart Tolle. In the book Eckhart says, "Am I the voice in my head? No, the voice in my head is not who I am. Who am I then? The one who sees that."

The voice in our head is known to send messages which are not good. The tape may be saying words that center on the ideas that:

> "You are unacceptable."
> "You need more."
> "You are not enough."

Some of my mind tapes playing quietly in the background were, and still can be, very damaging. They said things like:

> "You're so fat."
> "They think you are weird."
> "Can't you get anything right?"
> "You will never amount to anything."

These messages were developed by some of the people and experiences in my life. Media trained my body image. Some teachers taught me to feel shame. Parents and other authority figures instilled in me I am to be seen and not heard.

Check your thoughts often and listen closely to what your mind is saying. Make sure to question if what your mind is saying is true.

TRACKING PROGRESS - WEEK TWO

THE VOICE IN YOUR HEAD							
LISTEN CLOSELY TO YOUR SELF TALK TO SEE WHAT MESSAGES YOU ARE SENDING YOUR WAY.							
	SUN	MON	TUES	WED	THUR	FRI	SAT
MAKE YOUR BED							
GRATITUDE/JOY JOURNAL							
THE VOICE IN YOUR HEAD							

Sunday through Saturday

In the same way you learned to catch yourself thinking, you can check to see what the voice in your head is saying.

At each of your scheduled check in times, note what message you are sending yourself.

Is it positive?

True?

Joyous?

JOURNAL PAGE

13 WEEK SCHEDULE -WEEK TWO

THE VOICE IN YOUR HEAD							
LISTEN CLOSELY TO YOUR SELF TALK TO SEE WHAT MESSAGES YOU ARE SENDING YOUR WAY.							
	SUN	MON	TUES	WED	THUR	FRI	SAT
MAKE YOUR BED							
GRATITUDE/JOY JOURNAL							
THE VOICE IN YOUR HEAD							

GRATITUDES   JOY
MONDAY
1.   1.
2.   2.
3.   3.
4.   4.
5.   5.

TUESDAY
1.   1.
2.   2.
3.   3.
4.   4.
5.   5.

WEDNESDAY
1.   1.
2.   2.
3.   3.
4.   4.
5.   5.

THURSDAY
1.   1.
2.   2.
3.   3.
4.   4.
5.   5.

GRATITUDES   JOY
FRIDAY
1.   1.
2.   2.
3.   3.
4.   4.
5.   5.

SATURDAY
1.   1.
2.   2.
3.   3.
4.   4.
5.   5.

SUNDAY
1.   1.
2.   2.
3.   3.
4.   4.
5.   5.

MORE IN DEPTH TRACKING
SUNDAY THROUGH SATURDAY

THE VOICE IN YOUR HEAD							
LISTEN CLOSELY TO YOUR SELF TALK TO SEE WHAT MESSAGES YOU ARE SENDING YOUR WAY.							
	SUN	MON	TUES	WED	THUR	FRI	SAT
MAKE YOUR BED							
GRATITUDE/JOY JOURNAL							
THE VOICE IN YOUR HEAD							

During this week pay close attention to what you say to yourself.

Is it positive (pos), true, or negative (neg)?

SUNDAY

THE VOICE IN MY HEAD IS SAYING…	POS	TRUE	NEG

MONDAY

THE VOICE IN MY HEAD IS SAYING...	POS	TRUE	NEG

TUESDAY

THE VOICE IN MY HEAD IS SAYING...	POS	TRUE	NEG

WEDNESDAY

THE VOICE IN MY HEAD IS SAYING...	POS	TRUE	NEG

THURSDAY

THE VOICE IN MY HEAD IS SAYING...	POS	TRUE	NEG

FRIDAY

THE VOICE IN MY HEAD IS SAYING...	POS	TRUE	NEG

SATURDAY

THE VOICE IN MY HEAD IS SAYING...	POS	TRUE	NEG

XI. WEEK THREE - IS THAT TRUE?

As you inquire into issues and turn judgements around, you come to see that every perceived problem appearing "out there" is really nothing more than a misperception within your own thinking.
Byron Katie

One of the best ways to retool our negative life view and therefore GET A GRIP, is to carefully decide what is true. Because we like to believe the worst is happening, it is important for us to scrutinize our thoughts and search for false thinking. By being present, listening and communicating, I learned to stop myself and ask the question, "Is what I am thinking actually true?" The answer is almost always no. I go on to ask myself, "Even if it was true, can I do anything about it right now? Again, the answer is almost always no. I would finally remind myself, "Why not wait until you know for sure what has happened before you make yourself sick with worry." My personal example for this comes from my children taking the wheel and driving on their own. I worried needlessly that they would get in an accident and be hurt, and I would waste hours doing this before their scheduled return. In the end, when the kids actually came home, none of what I worried about was true.

With practice, I became fairly good at not walking down the worry path of no return. Notice I said fairly. Maintaining good thinking takes consistent effort.

IS WHAT I AM THINKING TRUE?

Asking "Is that true?" is a very simple technique to control thoughts and counteract our brain's predisposition to make up issues to work on. When I ask myself, "Is that true?" I test my thinking to see if it is valid. Each time I establish there is no proof, I go on to ask myself, "Do I want to waste what is true (the present moment) on what likely isn't real, and spoil the beautiful time that is?" The answer is always NO.

Whenever you have a negative thought, ask yourself, "Is that true?" Capture one single thought and get facts to support whether what you think is true or not. If you can't gather any facts, you know you are on the path of no return.

And do this with your loved ones. They are preprogrammed to think negative thoughts just as you are. When they come to you and tell you a problem, you can use it as a teaching moment. Gently guide them to notice their thoughts by quizzing them about what they were thinking when the issue happened. This isn't easy for them, and they will need some help getting to the root thought. Once they can, then teach them to ask themselves, "Is that true?"

A common problem for all of us, and especially children, is based on friends. For example, children will often be upset by something someone said at school. A child might say to your child, "You are weird." This will create all sorts of thoughts that your child can think. But the bottom line is to determine if what the child said is true. The answer is no, of course they aren't weird. But this is also a time to talk about social skills, how we present ourselves, and whether your child is trying too hard to be who they are not.

90

Why did the other child say "You're weird" when it isn't even true? That is a topic for a whole other book.

Asking "Is that true?" is a very simple technique to control thoughts and counteract our brain's predisposition to make up issues to work on. As you check your thoughts, ask "Is what I am thinking actually true?" Then ask, "Even if it was true, can I do anything about it right now? Finally remind yourself, "Why not wait until you know for sure what has happened before you make yourself sick with worry."

Add this to your system, routine, and small first steps of catching yourself thinking.

TRACKING PROGRESS - WEEK THREE

IS THAT TRUE?							
CHECK YOUR THOUGHT OFTEN TO ASCERTAIN IF YOUR THINKING IS TRUE							
	SUN	MON	TUES	WED	THUR	FRI	SAT
MAKE YOUR BED							
GRATITUDE/JOY JOURNAL							
IS THAT TRUE?							

Sunday – Are you honest with yourself about how you spend your time? Do you analyze what you do and when you do it? Check your weekly schedule and look at how you spend your time, then ask yourself if that is in line with what you thought you were doing.

Monday – As you head out to do what you do on Monday; what things are you thinking? Are you thinking today will be hard? Are you worried that someone is mad? Whichever thoughts you are creating in your mind, be sure to prove them correct or false.

Tuesday – As you make it through day two of this week, look for patterns in your thinking. Are you often wrong in your assumptions? Remember to ask "is that true" to clarify if what you read, heard or thought is false.

Wednesday – This is hump day, or is it? When thinking through this commonly held view of a Wednesday, are we making assumptions about every person's work week? Even simple thoughts need some attention, don't they?

Thursday – Do you read emails from friends, acquaintances, or co-workers that quote a statistic or contain an opinion and stop to question "is that true?" If you don't, today is a great day to start.

Friday – As you complete five days of work, review your actions and how you go about accomplishing tasks and ask yourself, how can I do better? How can I be more efficient? And is my opinion of how well I am doing true? Does it work in my favor?

Saturday – Host a family meeting to learn if how you believe things are going is actually how others in your family feel. "Is that true" questions work in all sorts of situations.

JOURNAL PAGE

13 WEEK SCHEDULE -WEEK THREE

IS THAT TRUE?							
CHECK YOUR THOUGHT OFTEN TO ASCERTAIN IF YOUR THINKING IS TRUE							
	SUN	MON	TUES	WED	THUR	FRI	SAT
MAKE YOUR BED							
GRATITUDE/JOY JOURNAL							
IS THAT TRUE?							

GRATITUDES   JOY

MONDAY
1.   1.
2.   2.
3.   3.
4.   4.
5.   5.

TUESDAY
1.   1.
2.   2.
3.   3.
4.   4.
5.   5.

WEDNESDAY
1.   1.
2.   2.
3.   3.
4.   4.
5.   5.

THURSDAY
1.   1.
2.   2.
3.   3.
4.   4.
5.   5.

GRATITUDES   JOY

FRIDAY
1.   1.
2.   2.
3.   3.
4.   4.
5.   5.

SATURDAY
1.   1.
2.   2.
3.   3.
4.   4.
5.   5.

SUNDAY
1.   1.
2.   2.
3.   3.
4.   4.
5.   5.

MORE IN DEPTH WORK
SUNDAY THROUGH SATURDAY

IS THAT TRUE?							
CHECK YOUR THOUGHT OFTEN TO ASCERTAIN IF YOUR THINKING IS TRUE							
	SUN	MON	TUES	WED	THUR	FRI	SAT
MAKE YOUR BED							
GRATITUDE/JOY JOURNAL							
IS THAT TRUE?							

Sunday

Are you honest with yourself about how you spend your time? Do you believe you have too much to do when really that isn't true? Check your weekly schedule and look at how you spend your time.

DAY	TIME OF DAY	WHAT ARE YOU DOING?

Monday

As you head out to do what you do on Monday, what things are you thinking? Are you thinking today will be hard? Are you worried that someone is mad? Whichever thoughts you are creating in your mind, be sure to prove them correct or false.

MONDAY MORNING

WHAT ARE YOUR ASSUMPTIONS?	TRUE OR FALSE?

Tuesday

As you make it through day two of this week, look for patterns in your thinking. Are you often wrong in your assumptions? Remember to ask "is that true" to clarify if what you read, heard or thought is false.

TIME	WHAT ARE YOU DOING?	WHAT ARE YOUR ASSUMPTIONS?

Wednesday

This is hump day, or is it? Are we making assumptions about every person's work week? Even simple thoughts and beliefs need some scrutiny.

Time	What are you doing?	What are your assumptions?

Thursday

Do you read emails or view social media posts from friends, acquaintances, or co-workers that quote a statistic or contain an opinion and stop to question "is that true?" If you don't, today is a great day to start.

Time	What are you doing?	What are your assumptions?

Friday

As you complete five days of work, review your actions and how you go about accomplishing tasks. Ask yourself if how you see your productivity is true. Ask yourself, how can I do better? How can I be more efficient? And is my opinion of how well I am doing true? Does it work in my favor?

Time	What are you doing?	What are your assumptions?

Saturday

Do you hold assumptions about how a Saturday "should be"? Are weekends really different from weekdays? "Is that true" questions work in all sorts of situations.

Time	What are you doing?	What are your assumptions?

XII.   WEEK FOUR - NEGATIVE THINKING

NEGATIVE NEUTRAL POSITIVE

The patterns of our lives reveal us. Our habits measure us.
Mary Oliver

Most of the work we need to do on our thinking involves retooling or discarding our thoughts, but mostly retooling. When you GET A GRIP, you retool your thoughts for better feelings and more appropriate responses. And to get beyond negative repetitive thinking you need to remember just because you think a thought doesn't mean it is true, so why not choose thoughts that get the best result?

NEGATIVE REPETITIVE THINKING

We are caught in an infinite loop of negative, repetitive thoughts which aren't necessarily valid. Our brain likes to believe people are out to get us, that life is hard, and we are being used, just in case it is the truth, so we are prepared. And because our brain wants us to survive, when we decide to believe something is true, our brain will make sure it is. Yet what we believe is what we decide is true, not necessarily what actually is, and the responsibility of deciding what to believe rests solely on our shoulders.

To explain this, I will use "spring cleaning" as an example.

Culturally, we have been taught to spring clean, and not just in the spring. In our modern society we have plenty, and often too much. Over the course of a single year, but definitely over the course of our life, we accumulate many items which we started out believing were essential, only to learn later we don't use nor need them, so we "spring clean". If you, like me, have read about perfecting this process, while going through your closets, drawers, garages, etc. you know you must decide which pile each item belongs in, keep, donate, or throw away.

Clutter in our mind is like the clutter in our drawers, and as a wise nun was known to say, when your drawers are in order, your soul is in order. For our thinking to be in order, we must decide whether to keep, donate, or throw away our thoughts and when talking about our thinking I like to label the piles as keep, retool, or discard.

As we go through our belongings and choose to believe, "I might need that" and then keep the item even though we could easily get rid of it, each time we use it, the voice in our head will validate that we did in fact "need" it. The reality is we could decide we don't need it, throw it away and our brain would validate that idea too.

WHAT WE BELIEVE

The same is true for our thoughts, our brain will make what we believe true. If we learned to believe things are scarce, and decided that is true, we tend to keep things. If we learned to believe that we have plenty, which is my mantra, and decided that is true, we can give things away.

Most of the work we do on our thinking involves retooling and discarding, but mostly retooling. The biggest reason for spring cleaning our thoughts is because thoughts create feelings and feelings turn into actions; what we do originates in what we think. It works like this:

You are driving down the road and someone cuts you off.

You think – that jerk just cut me off.

Your thought creates a feeling – you get mad, maybe even enraged.

Your feeling causes you to react – you shout out "jerk" or some other choice words to the person, use a finger signal to communicate your displeasure through the windshield, are caught off guard by the amount of frustration in your body, and feel ticked off for the rest of the day.

The jerk label you assign to this bad driver may or may not be true - you don't know this person so you can't be sure.

We can easily become emotionally overwhelmed by our thoughts and then blindsided by our actions. But that is not what I want for you or your loved ones.

Let's rework my example above and show how, when you GET A GRIP, you can retool your thoughts for better feelings and more appropriate responses.

You are driving down the road and someone cuts you off.

You choose to think – they must need to be in a hurry.

Your thought creates a feeling – you feel compassion for the other person.

Your feeling causes you to react – you wish them well and go about your day.

You don't know if either of the thoughts you created in your head, jerk or in a hurry, are necessarily true, so why not choose to think the thought that gets the best result?

To change how we act, we must take time to sort through our thoughts. Once we do, we need to determine which "pile" our thoughts belong in - keep, retool, or discard. Retooling the "what a jerk" thought into "they must need to be in a hurry" works best because it creates a better feeling and action. Determining which pile takes practice, but just like spring cleaning, it is worth the effort.

Due to old DNA we tend to view life through the dark lens of negativity. We keep certain beliefs and the voice in our head maintains them with a silent thought stream. To GET A GRIP we must retool the negative repetitive way we view life. Often this retooling is accomplished by making a simple shift, as with our what a jerk example, in our thought patterns.

Let me give you an example. I heard a story recently about a man who decided to say yes to opportunities that came his way for an entire year. When he did, his whole life changed for the better. I easily related to this "say yes" idea because of a life changing experience I had several years ago which I continue to use today. This experience involves saying "yes, and".

Educators often have workshop days and my experience on one of these days involved saying "yes and". We were to sign up for classes taught by our colleagues, and we were instructed to choose things that were out of our comfort zone so we could relate to and remember what it feels like to be a student.

I chose Improv. I was extremely nervous because, in my youth, I was taught to avoid failure – being wrong is not an option, and not knowing anything about Improv, I was certain to fail. But I wanted to take advantage of every opportunity that comes my way, so I pushed myself.

YES AND

Improv uses the strategy of "yes, and". While in a skit with another actor, you respond to anything they present with a "yes" and then you add on to it with an "and". This seems so simple, but in practice it takes some work. My first improv skit involved working with a partner who started our scene by asking me for five dollars. I killed the scene by responding, I don't have any money. That was not a "yes and", it was a "no but" and it fell flat. Luckily, after several attempts I was able to get the gist of agreeing to the made-up plot and adding to it. With practice I calmed down and was able to listen more carefully. I only allowed myself to agree with whatever was said. By doing so I opened up the possibility for me to add something to the scene.

I decided I would use "yes, and" as a mantra in my life. The "yes, and" strategy of Improv is all based on listening, communicating and being in the moment. When we focus on what is actually happening rather than what we think is going on, and we listen to what people are actually saying rather than thinking about what we will say, and ask clarifying questions to be able to say "yes, and", we experience life as it is rather than the dark lens view we normally have. Saying yes doesn't mean I believe everything is true and good. It just means I accept what others are saying, I will listen, and then add to the conversation.

One of my workshop attendees used this technique in a different context while talking with her spouse. As he was working through his thoughts out loud with her, she would normally say "no and" which would lead to him shutting down or them having an argument. But once she learned about "yes and" she decided she would use it instead which allowed him to feel heard and ended in both being much happier.

TRACKING PROGRESS - WEEK FOUR

NEGATIVE THINKING							
EACH TIME YOUR THINK SOMETHING NEGATIVE TURN IT INTO OTHER THOUGHTS CENTERED ON POSITIVITY AND TRUTH							
	SUN	MON	TUES	WED	THUR	FRI	SAT
MAKE YOUR BED							
GRATITUDE/JOY JOURNAL							
NEGATIVE THINKING							

Sunday through Saturday

Chart whether your thoughts are negative, neutral, or positive. You can use something like what I provided below.

Look for patterns of time or situations which cause you to have a negative focus. At the end of the week, look at times of day, and what was happening to understand what irritates you so in the future you will be able to prepare mentally and emotionally for upcoming experiences.

	MORNING THOUGHTS ARE NEU, POS, NEG?	AFTERNOON THOUGHTS ARE NEU, POS, NEG?	EVENING THOUGHTS ARE NEU, POS, NEG?
SUNDAY			
MONDAY			
TUESDAY			
WEDNESDAY			
THURSDAY			
FRIDAY			
SATURDAY			

JOURNAL PAGE

13 WEEK SCHEDULE -WEEK FOUR

NEGATIVE THINKING							
EACH TIME YOUR THINK SOMETHING NEGATIVE TURN IT INTO OTHER THOUGHTS CENTERED ON POSITIVITY AND TRUTH							
	SUN	MON	TUES	WED	THUR	FRI	SAT
MAKE YOUR BED							
GRATITUDE/JOY JOURNAL							
NEGATIVE THINKING							

GRATITUDES   JOY

MONDAY
1.   1.
2.   2.
3.   3.
4.   4.
5.   5.

TUESDAY
1.   1.
2.   2.
3.   3.
4.   4.
5.   5.

WEDNESDAY
1.   1.
2.   2.
3.   3.
4.   4.
5.   5.

THURSDAY
1.   1.
2.   2.
3.   3.
4.   4.
5.   5.

GRATITUDES   JOY

FRIDAY
1.   1.
2.   2.
3.   3.
4.   4.
5.   5.

SATURDAY
1.   1.
2.   2.
3.   3.
4.   4.
5.   5.

SUNDAY
1.   1.
2.   2.
3.   3.
4.   4.
5.   5.

MORE IN DEPTH TRACKING
SUNDAY THROUGH SATURDAY

NEGATIVE THINKING							
EACH TIME YOUR THINK SOMETHING NEGATIVE TURN IT INTO OTHER THOUGHTS CENTERED ON POSITIVITY AND TRUTH							
	SUN	MON	TUES	WED	THUR	FRI	SAT
MAKE YOUR BED							
GRATITUDE/JOY JOURNAL							
NEGATIVE THINKING							

As you focus on your individual thoughts, chart whether your thoughts are negative (NEG), neutral (NEU), or positive (POS). Even if you only have time to do this once or twice a day it will be enough to help you realize the type of thoughts you tend to have.

Look for patterns of time or situations which cause you to have a negative focus. At the end of the week, look at times of day, and what was happening to understand what irritates you so in the future you will be able to prepare mentally and emotionally for upcoming experiences. More on that later.

SUNDAY

TIME/PLACE	THOUGHT	NEG	NEU	POS

MONDAY

TIME/PLACE	THOUGHT	NEG	NEU	POS

TUESDAY

TIME/PLACE	THOUGHT	NEG	NEU	POS

WEDNESDAY

TIME/PLACE	THOUGHT	NEG	NEU	POS

THURSDAY

TIME/PLACE	THOUGHT	NEG	NEU	POS

FRIDAY

TIME/PLACE	THOUGHT	NEG	NEU	POS

SATURDAY

TIME/PLACE	THOUGHT	NEG	NEU	POS

XIII. WEEK FIVE - LIMITING BELIEFS

Do the uncomfortable. Become comfortable with these acts. Prove to yourself that your limiting beliefs die a quick death if you will simply do what you feel uncomfortable doing.
Darren Rowse

A barrier to making any change is that you talk yourself into believing things that limit you. You believe you can't, so you don't even start. Or you think the change will take too much time and effort, so you give up before trying.

THOUGHTS HOLD US BACK

We all have thoughts that aren't true, and generally they don't do much to us other than waste our time, but some are actually harmful. We create damaging emotions as we complain, think others are better than we are, and judge people and situations for not being as they "should be". The worst part of it all is that these emotions are based solely on the stuff we tell ourselves via the voice in our head and they hold us back.

In a previous chapter, I told you that during childhood we made up reasons for circumstances which weren't true because our thinking was "faulty". Other times we were taught to believe things that weren't true by the people in our lives. These thoughts run silently in the back of our minds, and for the most part, are undetectable. Yet, they guide what we think and feel, and thus, how we act. When what we learned to believe holds us back from fully reaching our promise and potential, these thoughts are known as limiting beliefs and they need to be discarded.

Limiting beliefs can easily get in our way. Some of the tough spots in our lives are actually created by our own limiting beliefs. We might, without realizing it, think that nothing works out for us or life is out to get us. Or we might believe other people have more luck than we do. When life gets hard, we tend to think we are the only one suffering, right? Thinking in this limiting way is definitely not to our advantage.

You might be wondering what thoughts you have that are holding you back.

Recall that we all have similar worries and concerns, so let me give you some probable suspects for your limiting beliefs.

- I must go to college to be successful
- Everyone needs to date a lot before they get married
- It's who you know, not what you know
- Money can't buy happiness
- It will take too long to …
- You should be married by 30 and have two children
- You are really successful when you make $_____
- You can retire when you have _____ dollars
- I must have a lot of information to make a decision
- I am lucky to even have a job
- People are just born that way

·   I'm just not good at...

One of the biggest limiting thoughts we think is that other people's lives are much better than ours.

It isn't surprising that we think everyone else is so much better off than we are because our old DNA brain loves to berate us and constantly test whether we are worthy. But as we dig a little deeper, we realize that others are just like we are. Everyone struggles at times and feels overwhelmed. Even your most put together colleague, whom you see as semi-perfect, has his/her off days.

To overcome the limiting beliefs which are obstacles to GET A GRIP, we must delve deep into what we think, recognize which thoughts are false and therefore hold us back, and prove our limiting beliefs wrong. We do this by looking for the basis for what we are thinking.

Maybe the kid who always wore stripes picked on you at school. You concluded that anyone who wears stripes is mean and now as a grownup (without realizing it) you shy away from stripes altogether. Simplified example, I know, but you get the idea.

Our limiting beliefs not only make us uneasy about people, places, and things, they can also wreak havoc with our self-image. Let me give you an example.

When I was young, as my anxiety started to come to the forefront, no one understood much about being worried all the time and I learned the limiting belief that being anxious was a bad quality and I should toughen up. I desperately wanted to be tough, not worried, but I didn't have the tools. I wanted to be normal, just like everyone else, and I believed no one else had any problems. I berated myself for who I was. Over the years, I have been able to prove my limiting belief wrong and view my anxiety as a blessing. I came to realize that because of my anxiety, I have heightened awareness, therefore I can feel what others are feeling and more easily connect with them. I am driven internally to help others, so being able to feel what they're feeling has upped my ability to assist them. Instead of hating the fact

116

that I am anxious, I learned to make it a part of me, learn to manage it, and welcome it as something about me that most of the time works well. I have taught this view of anxiety to many students who struggle with feeling anxious. Adjusting their limiting belief, even if just a little bit as I did, helped them view their inherent traits as a blessing rather than a curse. You too might need to tweak your thoughts about who you are and the qualities you have.

I SHOULDN'T

On our path to GET A GRIP we must work on our many limiting beliefs, which isn't a one-time exercise and doesn't happen all at once. In the last couple of years, I heard another one of my long-standing limiting thoughts, which surprised me, because I thought I had dealt with all of them (hahaha, another limiting belief). The thought I was thinking was I shouldn't go out too much at night during the week. When I actually heard myself think this, I was stunned. I am more than old enough and very able at this stage in my life to do as I please. My children are grown, I can afford to go out, and I have the time to do so.

While working to prove this thought wrong, I asked myself, "Why not go out every night of the week if I want to?" I thought about the root cause for this limiting belief and realized it came from being raised by parents who survived the great depression, 1929 - 1933. My mum and dad always preached that we must keep the wolf from the door. If you don't know what that means, and I can understand easily that you might not because it is a weird old saying, let me explain. The wolf is based on the bad character in the story of *The Three Little Pigs*. If you haven't read this book, please know it has taken on new meaning in today's world. My wolf is based on the story from the 1950s and 60s in which two of the pigs weren't able to build good homes. They end up in their industrious brother's house which is built of bricks that can withstand anything the wolf tries to do to get in to eat them.

When my parents used the saying, keep the wolf from the door, they were referring to being lazy, or frivolous, and getting oneself to a place where you don't have enough money, food, housing, etc. So, to keep the wolf from your door it is important to work hard, prepare thoroughly, and not be wasteful - like going out every night of the week. When I got to the bottom of this belief, I was able to completely understand why I hesitate. But I realized I can make good decisions, such as whether or not I have the means to go out every single night of each week if I want to. Do I go out every night of the week? No, but I don't have the feeling that I can't.

PROVE LIMITING BELIEFS WRONG

As I mentioned, to rid ourselves of limiting beliefs, those thoughts that aren't true and hold us back, we must first hear them and then prove them wrong. Here are a couple of my personal examples of limiting thoughts and how I changed them.

I learned to believe that being overly enthusiastic or excited is unacceptable. This idea developed when I was young because the mantra of that day was "Children are to be seen and not heard." In my household, during the timeframe I was raised, it was expected that we control ourselves at all times, especially in public. So even now, when I get "out of control" by being super excited (and I get this way often), I initially feel embarrassed and must remind myself I don't have to be.

One of my all-time most ridiculous limiting beliefs was speeding will make up for lost time and by going faster I can avoid being late. Have you ever noticed that when you are running behind schedule you speed to get there on time? We all do. In order to combat this limiting thought, and as the math person I am, I calculated the way this works in order to prove this limiting belief wrong and talk myself out of speeding (at least in terms of being late).

As an example, let's pretend you're going to be ten minutes late for a 9 A.M. appointment if you drive the speed limit (45mph). Your appointment is 10 miles away. So, you decide to speed, thinking it will help you to arrive on time. But the truth lies in the numbers.

Let's calculate these numbers to validate or refute whether or not speeding will make up the time.

Driving 45 miles per hour (the speed limit) means you will get there in 10 miles divided by 45 miles/hour which is .222222 hours or 13 1/3 minutes.

This means if you left your house just before 8:57AM (your morning was chaotic) you would arrive at your appointment at 9:10AM.

Now, if you drive 55 miles per hour (ten miles per hour over the speed limit) you will get there in 10/55 or .181818 hours or 10.9 minutes (round it to 11 mins for ease of calculating).

That means leaving just before 8:57AM you will arrive at roughly 9:08AM. Still eight minutes late.

Driving 10mph over the speed limit gains you two minutes, but not enough to arrive on time, and will definitely gain the attention of any law enforcement. When they get a hold of you, you will be much later. Better to call and say you are running 10 minutes late and drive the speed limit, right?

Similar to this limiting belief is thinking it is better to drive across town to save three cents per gallon of gas rather than fill up at the corner station. Let's work through this example too. We will use my car to do the math. My gas tank holds a total of 10 gallons, so three cents cheaper and 10 gallons means I would save 30 cents by driving across town to fill up. But, since driving across town means I drive 10 miles, and my car gets 30 miles to the gallon, I will use 1/3 of a gallon of gas just getting to the other gas station. A gallon costs roughly $3.00 per gallon so I spent $1.00 to drive across town to save a total of 30 cents. See what I mean when I say limiting beliefs?

Even though I know all this, I still have a strong desire to make up the time or save a few cents, but each time the thought arises I recognize my faulty limiting thoughts and fight them hard.

Some of the biggest limiting beliefs we hold onto center on being worthy. We are convinced everyone notices what we do, what we wear, what we say, who our friends are, when in reality they don't. We learned these thoughts from our culture and upbringing. As children we learned not only from our parent(s), but also from society. Most childhood limiting beliefs are based on the "I am not worthy" worries.

When you were a child, your limiting beliefs may have involved thoughts like:

- Friends will like me if I am cool and always do the right thing
- I can't get a good grade because the teacher hates me
- I am not athletic (even though the reason is that they don't practice)
- I am not good at math (English, art, etc. even though this is due to the fact they don't put in the work)

And as we aged, we may have continued these beliefs. For all of us to GET A GRIP and reach our promise and potential, we must work on controlling our limiting beliefs. We do this by proving them wrong, by remembering that just because we think a thought doesn't mean it is true, and by creating replacement beliefs that are accurate and in line with our goals. This work is heavy lifting. First, because we don't notice our thinking, and second, because we want to believe what we have decided is true, even though it isn't. Recall that thoughts create feelings which then turn into actions. To get the best response we need to choose the best thought, which certainly isn't one that is limiting our behavior.

Let me give you a prime example. Imagine me waking in the morning. It is raining outside. I hate rain and the sunless skies that come with it. Because of this I immediately think, "I won't have a great day because it is raining and gloomy outside." In my mind, I have decided to believe that is how my day will be. Because I think this thought, sadness creeps into my soul. But is what I am thinking true? Will I have a terrible day? Am I sad? When I look for the truth in my thoughts, I can't find any. So, I work to shake off my negative thoughts by seeing the moment as it is. It's overcast outside. No judgement, just fact. And rain has no impact on my day other than I need to dress for it by not wearing my good shoes (I don't want to get them wet). With this new thought, my gloom is gone, and I feel better. I am not deciding how things will be, I am enjoying what is.

Just because you think a thought doesn't mean it is true and by creating replacement beliefs that are accurate and in line with your goals, you can reach your promise and potential.

Check in with your thoughts often. Listen for your limiting beliefs and hear what they are saying. Then grab them tight and decide if they are worth keeping, if you need to retool them, or if you can discard them entirely.

To prove your limiting thoughts wrong, check to see if your belief is true. When you ask, "Is that true?" and find nothing supports your thought, like my speeding example, it is easier to move beyond your limiting belief.

Some limiting, faulty thinking will not go away entirely. But as with me, you can recognize it, catch it early before it ruins your day, and change the thought for a better one.

System – Question what you believe. It is usually when you are making a decision that your limiting beliefs rise up and show their true colors. When going about your day, whether at home, at work, with family or with friends, you might get a feeling like "I shouldn't" or you feel hesitant. When that happens, you need to analyze why you feel like hesitating or stopping.

Routine – When you are making a decision of any kind, question on what you are basing your thoughts. Listen for the limiting belief and ask yourself, is that true?

Think of the famous Aesop Fable, The Tortoise and the Hare.

The moral of that story is it is better to do things slow and steady; you will be more successful doing them that way rather than being quick and careless. Have you ever said this to yourself while trying to support your slowness? But is it true that slow and steady wins the race, especially when talking about life?

Small first step – Start with one limiting belief and prove it wrong. Replace the limiting belief with a new, more positive, and true belief.

TRACKING PROGRESS - WEEK FIVE

LIMITING BELIEFS							
IS WHAT YOU ARE THINKING AND BELIEVING HOLDING YOU BACK? IS IT TRUE?　CAN YOU PROVE IT?							
	SUN	MON	TUES	WED	THUR	FRI	SAT
MAKE YOUR BED							
GRATITUDE/JOY JOURNAL							
LIMITING BELIEFS							

Sunday through Saturday

Each day as you make decisions try to get to the bottom of what made you decide the way you did. Was there a limiting belief driving your thoughts in a particular direction? When you locate your limiting beliefs, start making a list and then prove them wrong when necessary.

JOURNAL PAGE

13 WEEK SCHEDULE -WEEK FIVE

LIMITING BELIEFS								
IS WHAT YOU ARE THINKING AND BELIEVING HOLDING YOU BACK? IS IT TRUE? CAN YOU PROVE IT?								
	SUN	MON	TUES	WED	THUR	FRI	SAT
MAKE YOUR BED								
GRATITUDE/JOY JOURNAL								
LIMITING BELIEFS								

GRATITUDES   JOY

MONDAY
1.   1.
2.   2.
3.   3.
4.   4.
5.   5.

TUESDAY
1.   1.
2.   2.
3.   3.
4.   4.
5.   5.

WEDNESDAY
1.   1.
2.   2.
3.   3.
4.   4.
5.   5.

THURSDAY
1.   1.
2.   2.
3.   3.
4.   4.
5.   5.

GRATITUDES   JOY

FRIDAY
1.   1.
2.   2.
3.   3.
4.   4.
5.   5.

SATURDAY
1.   1.
2.   2.
3.   3.
4.   4.
5.   5.

SUNDAY
1.   1.
2.   2.
3.   3.
4.   4.
5.   5.

MORE IN DEPTH TRACKING
SUNDAY THROUGH SATURDAY

LIMITING BELIEFS							
IS WHAT YOU ARE THINKING AND BELIEVING HOLDING YOU BACK? IS IT TRUE? CAN YOU PROVE IT?							
	SUN	MON	TUES	WED	THUR	FRI	SAT
MAKE YOUR BED							
GRATITUDE/JOY JOURNAL							
LIMITING BELIEFS							

Each day as you make decisions try to get to the bottom of what made you decide the way you did. Was there a limiting belief driving your thoughts in a particular direction?

List the decisions you make each day along with your limiting beliefs, determine if they are T (true) or F (false), and when false, prove them wrong.

SUNDAY

DECISION	LIMITING BELIEF	T	F

MONDAY

DECISION	LIMITING BELIEF	T	F

TUESDAY

DECISION	LIMITING BELIEF	T	F

WEDNESDAY

DECISION	LIMITING BELIEF	T	F

THURSDAY

DECISION	LIMITING BELIEF	T	F

FRIDAY

DECISION	LIMITING BELIEF	T	F

SATURDAY

DECISION	LIMITING BELIEF	T	F

XIV.   WEEK SIX - FEAR

He who is not every day conquering some fear has not learned the secret of life."
Ralph Waldo Emerson

Just as we did with "What a jerk", we easily assume people don't like us, that everyone can see our flaws, that there isn't enough to go around, and the list goes on. We like to fear, as if in order to be ready and able to survive, this is what life demands. And our biggest fear is that of failure.

The remarkable thing about all of our fear is that most of what we fear is based on what we make up in our mind. We fabricate thoughts and then tell ourselves they are true. We even make them feel real, and this makes sense because fear of something real and fear of something we create in our mind feels the same in our body.

Fear is a large obstacle to overcome in order to GET A GRIP because it drives most of our negative thought processes. We fear losing a loved one, whether we remember to do something, how our children are doing, if we are healthy, meeting with our boss, flying... and the fear we create for ourselves consumes us and feels very real, even when it isn't. Because I want you and your loved ones to reach your highest potential, and because fear can make us say no rather than "yes, and", I want to explain what I know about fear so you can remove this bump in the road.

FEAR OR EXCITEMENT

Fear of something real or fear of something we imagine is not the only mistake we make with what we feel. Most people don't know that fear and excitement feel the same way in the body too, so they believe they are afraid when really, they are excited. (It is the story we use to explain what we are feeling that decides whether it is fear or excitement.) I am not suggesting that we are never afraid, or shouldn't be, but often, for many opportunities which scare us, it is far better to be excited than afraid.

A great example of this is public speaking. Many people are afraid to speak to a group. They operate with a worst-case-scenario in their head and are overcome by dread. They are certain that public speaking will end in disaster and they will make a fool of themselves. Their fear of embarrassment and failure is so strong they can't overcome it. Instead of grabbing the opportunity to speak, they decide they are too afraid, which limits their potential, especially for advancement in the workplace, which often demands they are able to make presentations.

Taking advantage of an opportunity requires us to push ourselves. When I first started speaking to groups, I too, was scared to be alone on stage in front of a large gathering. In order to take advantage of this opportunity I had to GET A GRIP. To overcome feeling fear, I told myself the pit in my stomach was excitement. I prepared thoroughly and practiced many times on the exact place I would be speaking. While reading The Charisma Myth by Olivia Fox Cabane, I learned to feel excited by upping my energy level with a playlist of music and centering my thoughts on the positive. If you are grappling with this - and need to speak to a group - please move through the fear and just do it, you will be happy you did.

FEAR OF FAILURE

Fear of failure is a large thinking obstacle to all of us. Recently I learned about the acronym F.A.I.L. When you think about failing, I want you to use F.A.I.L. - which means first attempt in learning. Failure is part and parcel of the learning process. Remember you can't know everything and everyone has to learn. Often it helps to turn the table so when you are fearing failure, I want you to transfer your focus to how you feel when someone else fails after trying hard. When I see someone work hard over and over again and finally learn, it is my happiest moment. Working at something until you get it "right" shows me you are wanting to live your life to the fullest.

Fear arises when we aren't prepared because we feel uneasy and uncertain. Like when public speaking, I made sure I was very prepared so that fear could be kept at bay. One sure way to conquer fear is to set up routines that keep you organized and prepared. Structure your mornings, your evenings and your weekends so that you have the most organized, intentional routines that make sure you are prepared for what is coming next. For one of my routines, I use my dry erase marker to write down the most important tasks of my week on my bathroom mirror so that I see them morning and night and therefore remember what is ahead.

Morning routines usually involve having your necessary items ready and waiting for you to take them with you for your day.

Evening routines are best when they allow time for you to do what needs to be done and to have time for relaxation.

And weekend routines should involve some sort of fun and frivolity so that you refill your energy bucket for the week ahead.

Plan yours now by writing down some ideas and try them for a week to see if they work for you. If they do, live them daily, if not tweak them so they do.

Morning Routine

_____

_____

_____

_____

_____

_____

Evening Routine

_____

_____

_____

_____

_____

_____

Weekend Routine

_____

_____

_____

_____

_____

_____

TRACKING PROGRESS - WEEK SIX

FEAR							
EACH TIME YOU ARE AFRAID, CHECK TO SEE IF WHAT YOU FEAR IS REAL OR IF YOU ARE ACTUALLY EXCTIED							
	SUN	MON	TUES	WED	THUR	FRI	SAT
MAKE YOUR BED							
GRATITUDE/JOY JOURNAL							
FEAR							

Sunday through Saturday

Write down your fears when they occur. Note them on your phone or in some way that you can see the entire list at the end of the week. After seven days, review the things that make you afraid. Are they real? Or are they things based on your thoughts of What If?

Each time you feel fearful, ask yourself if it is something you created in your head, if it is truly fear, or could it be excitement.

Fear is a large obstacle to overcome in order to GET A GRIP because it drives most of our negative thought processes. One of our biggest fears is that we aren't in control. When we are organized, we aren't caught off guard, we know what is coming, and we have what we need when we need it. We don't feel the need to fear that we won't be ready.

132

JOURNAL PAGE

13 WEEK SCHEDULE -WEEK SIX

FEAR							
EACH TIME YOU ARE AFRAID, CHECK TO SEE IF WHAT YOU FEAR IS REAL OR IF YOU ARE ACTUALLY EXCTIED							
	SUN	MON	TUES	WED	THUR	FRI	SAT
MAKE YOUR BED							
GRATITUDE/JOY JOURNAL							
FEAR							

GRATITUDES   JOY

MONDAY

1.   1.
2.   2.
3.   3.
4.   4.
5.   5.

TUESDAY

1.   1.
2.   2.
3.   3.
4.   4.
5.   5.

WEDNESDAY

1.   1.
2.   2.
3.   3.
4.   4.
5.   5.

THURSDAY

1.   1.
2.   2.
3.   3.
4.   4.
5.   5.

GRATITUDES   JOY

FRIDAY

1.   1.
2.   2.
3.   3.
4.   4.
5.   5.

SATURDAY

1.   1.
2.   2.
3.   3.
4.   4.
5.   5.

SUNDAY

1.   1.
2.   2.
3.   3.
4.   4.
5.   5.

MORE IN DEPTH TRACKING
SUNDAY THROUGH SATURDAY

FEAR							
EACH TIME YOU ARE AFRAID, CHECK TO SEE IF WHAT YOU FEAR IS REAL OR IF YOU ARE ACTUALLY EXCTIED							
	SUN	MON	TUES	WED	THUR	FRI	SAT
MAKE YOUR BED							
GRATITUDE/JOY JOURNAL							
FEAR							

Write down your fears when they occur. Keep track of them so that you can see the list at the end of the week and review the things that make you afraid. Each time you notice you are feeling fear, decide if it is something you created in your head, if it is truly fear, or could it be excitement. Or is it based on thoughts of What If? Put a check in the column that applies.

SUNDAY

LIST OF EACH FEAR	WHAT IF?	REAL?	EXCITED?

MONDAY

LIST OF EACH FEAR	WHAT IF?	REAL?	EXCITED?

TUESDAY

LIST OF EACH FEAR	WHAT IF?	REAL?	EXCITED?

WEDNESDAY

LIST OF EACH FEAR	WHAT IF?	REAL?	EXCITED?

THURSDAY

LIST OF EACH FEAR	WHAT IF?	REAL?	EXCITED?

FRIDAY

LIST OF EACH FEAR	WHAT IF?	REAL?	EXCITED?

SATURDAY

LIST OF EACH FEAR	WHAT IF?	REAL?	EXCITED?

REVIEW YOUR LIST OF FEARS

Combine similar fears under one category. For instance, fear of the unknown might be fear of a meeting with a boss, something you said to a friend, etc. Then tally how many of your fears are real, based on what if or just excitement.

FEARS THIS WEEK	WHAT IF?	REAL?	EXCITED?
TOTALS			

XV.   WEEK SEVEN – WORRY, AND THEN WHAT?

Worry never robs tomorrow of its sorrow,
it only saps today of its joy.
Leo F. Buscaglia

Running neck and neck with fear in the race of not so good things we learned to do, especially while we were young, is worrying. Contemplating the worst is easy for us due to our inherited old DNA. We are preprogrammed to worry, fear, judge, and think negative thoughts all in the name of survival. But we perfected worry from watching and being with those closest to us. People we experienced in our young lives passed along ideas without awareness, a great example of intent versus impact. Parents want to do the best job they can, but many pass along unintended messages, I know I did because I didn't know then what I know now.

WHAT WILL THE NEIGHBORS THINK?

During my childhood, my mother was known to say, "What will the neighbors think?" All the mothers I knew said this. I learned to internalize this worry with ease. It all started with the lady who lived directly across from my childhood home on McKinley Ave. My sister and I referred to her as Mrs. Crabbitz, the nosey neighbor in my favorite T.V. show Bewitched. Nothing escaped her purview. She knew what time of day or night I did anything, and she had no problem reporting every detail to my mother, as if my mother wasn't aware. Let me assure you nothing escaped my mother and she knew exactly what went on well before the report from across the street (I am convinced the saying "eyes in the back of her head" started with my mother). Still, the worry about what Mrs. Crabbitz was thinking seemed to occupy my mother because she would often warn, "What will the neighbors think?" As a young child, I learned to believe this must be important and with little effort, adopted worrying about the opinions of others.

Worrying about what others think is not healthy and often makes us feel not worthy. Because I developed this type of worry early on in my life, I constantly felt judged and believed I never measured up. I was consumed by what other people thought of me, how I dressed, and the work I produced. I am convinced this was not the intended message, but it is definitely the impact of the words spoken during my upbringing.

Learning how to change my, "What will they think" thoughts began in university. I had reached the point where worrying about what other people thought of me and how I looked was impacting my health and happiness. I decided to seek the help of a counselor in the counseling department and met with one named Larry. As I look back at those days, and after the work I have done since then, I find it hard to believe I was consumed by these ideas, but I was.

Larry didn't totally understand my need for approval from others but explained an interesting fact, nonetheless. He said if you enter a room with 100 people, at best, 10 will notice you, and at most, one will remember you. What? Really? I was sure everyone noticed me, right? I tested his information on myself, focused on who I notice and remember, and quickly realized he was right. This small shift in my thinking helped me as well as the many students I have shared it with.

Counseling has been and continues to be a great resource for me, especially when I need(ed) help restructuring my thoughts. I am a big fan of CBT; Cognitive Behavioral Therapy whose goal is to change the way we think so we can change the way we feel. Think Get A Grip is based on CBT and my personal strategies.

To deal with worrying it helped me to know the basis for my thoughts so I could prove them wrong and think new ones. In terms of my appearance, I know my worries came from the media. During my youth, Twiggy was the supermodel. Her rail thin physique didn't help anyone's self-esteem, especially not mine. Body image didn't come from my family or friends, it came from the print media, movies and television, much as it does today.

Overcoming my obsession with physical appearance has taken adjusting my thoughts, and when I heard the lyrics of the song, "Everyone's Free" (to wear sunscreen) I felt like they were speaking directly to me. The song is sung (actually spoken) by Bas Luhrman. A link to listen is in the bibliography. The words for the lyrics originated June 1, 1997 when Mary Schmich, a Chicago Tribune columnist and Brenda Starr, a cartoonist, wrote a column entitled "Advice, like youth, probably just wasted on the young."

In the song it says,

> Enjoy the power and beauty of your youth. Oh, never mind; you will not understand the power and beauty of your youth until they have faded. But trust me, in 20 years you'll look back at photos of yourself and recall in a way you can't grasp now how much possibility lay before you and how fabulous you really looked...you are not as fat as you imagine.

> *Do NOT read beauty magazines, they will only*
> *make you feel ugly.*

I know exactly what these lyrics are saying. I didn't appreciate the power and beauty of my youth. But I have turned that around and I know when I am a lot older, I will look back on even today and realize the potential that surrounds me currently. I hope hearing these words helps you too.

WORRY DOESN'T CHANGE THE FUTURE

Another strategy to overcome the thinking obstacle of worry is to understand that most of what we worry about never happens, and the stuff that does, comes out of nowhere.

A saying that helped me understand this also came from the Sunscreen Song.

> *Don't worry about the future; or worry but know*
> *that worrying is as effective as trying to solve an*
> *algebra equation by chewing bubblegum. The*
> *real troubles in your life are apt to be things that*
> *never crossed your worried mind, the kind that*
> *blindside you at 4pm on some idle Tuesday*
> *afternoon.*

Think about the things you have worried about, especially the biggies. Have any of them actually happened? What about the things that actually did come up that were scary, overwhelming, etc.? Did you worry about those? I bet you didn't even think of such things. As I look back on my life, the big tribulations were not things I could ever have imagined would occur. By remembering this truth, I have been able to avoid wasting valuable time worrying (for the most part). And focusing on what I expect of myself, what brings me joy, and asking "Is that true?" helps recenter my thoughts every time.

The reason worries overtake us and cause us grief is that we keep our worries "out there", held at a distance, as if we are sure they will be too much for us to handle, so we don't want to get too close.

Just as I did with old DNA, I developed a theory about how worry works against us and what we can do to GET A GRIP. My theory is worry is like a closed door at the end of a long hallway. We don't want to open the door and go through to the other side for fear of not being able to handle whatever is there. We don't want to get too close so we hold our worries at a distance. We just stare at the door down the hall and hold onto our nebulous burdens and waste time worrying about what might be, rather than enjoying what is.

Let me give you one of my favorite closed doors of worry examples. Behind this door lie thoughts of death; not mine, but the death of those I love. I don't like the feeling of being sad. I think the sadness created by the death of those near and dear to me will be very overwhelming when it comes. And because of this I remain down the hall, a fair distance from the closed door, afraid to get too close, sure that my emotions will make me lose control.

Rationally, I know death is inevitable, and being prepared for losing a loved one isn't really possible, we must experience it when it happens. Even so, I let my mind wander to how sad I think I will be and try to imagine how much guilt and regret I will have for every single misstep I made with that person. (Yes, I live with this brain and it tends to be guilt-ridden) But I don't really go to the place I will actually be when death happens. I can't, because I don't know how it will feel, not only because I haven't yet experienced it, but also because I keep my real feelings on the other side of the door down the hall.

This image may be all mine, but the worry about what is to come isn't, it happens to the best of us. For any of us to reclaim the time we waste worrying, we must change our thoughts by going down the hall and through the door.

AND THEN WHAT

To work through any worried thoughts that keep me stuck I use, "And then what?" to force myself down the hall and behind the "door". I have used this technique with a lot of success, and it has worked well with everyone I've taught it to. I don't remember where I learned it, but I am thankful I have it in my mental tool belt.

Let me walk you through one such exercise so you can understand the idea.

I start with my actual thought – I am going to be so sad when _____ dies (me trying to prepare for the worst).

Immediately I ask myself – okay, so you're sad, and then what?

Answer - I will cry a lot

I ask myself again - okay, so you cry a lot, and then what?

I will feel a deep sadness within me

Okay, and then what?

I will never be happy again (worst case scenario, I am a star at thinking this way)

Okay, and then what?

I will not be fun to be around

Okay, and then what?

Everyone will leave me, and I will be alone (worst-case scenario)

Okay, and then what?

I will have to change to make new friends

At this point, I know I have gone through the door to the other side because I realize my worries won't destroy me. The sadness that comes with death will be hard, but I know in my heart I can do it, and the worries I have are mostly unreasonable. Not everyone is going to leave me, and I won't always be unhappy. Realistically, I will be sad, and deeply so. I will cry. But it won't be forever.

To overcome any negative, scary, worried thinking, go all the way down the hall, open the door, look behind it, and walk through to the other side. Once there, sit with your worries long enough to get to know them well, work through them, and realize they will not be the end of you.

TRACKING PROGRESS - WEEK SEVEN

AND THEN WHAT?							
EACH TIME YOU HAVE A LONG-LASTING WORRIED THOUGHT, GO THROUGH THE "AND THEN WHAT" EXERCISE							
	SUN	MON	TUES	WED	THUR	FRI	SAT
MAKE YOUR BED							
GRATITUDE/JOY JOURNAL							
AND THEN WHAT?							

Sunday through Saturday

Each time you note you are worrying, and especially for each episode of extended worry, use the "And Then What" exercise to work through your thoughts.

To recoup the time we lose by worrying, we must go all the way down the hall, open the door, look behind it, and walk through to the other side. Once there, we must get to know our worries well, work through them, and realize they will not be the end of us.

JOURNAL PAGE

13 WEEK SCHEDULE -WEEK SEVEN

AND THEN WHAT?							
EACH TIME YOU HAVE A LONG-LASTING WORRIED THOUGHT, GO THROUGH THE "AND THEN WHAT" EXERCISE							
	SUN	MON	TUES	WED	THUR	FRI	SAT
MAKE YOUR BED							
GRATITUDE/JOY JOURNAL							
AND THEN WHAT?							

GRATITUDES   JOY

MONDAY
1.   1.
2.   2.
3.   3.
4.   4.
5.   5.

TUESDAY
1.   1.
2.   2.
3.   3.
4.   4.
5.   5.

WEDNESDAY
1.   1.
2.   2.
3.   3.
4.   4.
5.   5.

THURSDAY
1.   1.
2.   2.
3.   3.
4.   4.
5.   5.

GRATITUDES   JOY

FRIDAY
1.   1.
2.   2.
3.   3.
4.   4.
5.   5.

SATURDAY
1.   1.
2.   2.
3.   3.
4.   4.
5.   5.

SUNDAY
1.   1.
2.   2.
3.   3.
4.   4.
5.   5.

MORE IN DEPTH TRACKING
SUNDAY THROUGH SATURDAY

AND THEN WHAT?							
EACH TIME YOU HAVE A LONG-LASTING WORRIED THOUGHT, GO THROUGH THE "AND THEN WHAT" EXERCISE							
	SUN	MON	TUES	WED	THUR	FRI	SAT
MAKE YOUR BED							
GRATITUDE/JOY JOURNAL							
AND THEN WHAT?							

Each time you note you are experiencing an episode of extended worry, list what is causing the worry and then use the "And Then What" exercise to work through your thoughts. When complete, place a check mark to note the completion of the And Then What exercise for each worry.

SUNDAY

WORRIES	AND THEN WHAT?

MONDAY

WORRIES	AND THEN WHAT?

TUESDAY

WORRIES	AND THEN WHAT?

WEDNESDAY

WORRIES	AND THEN WHAT?

THURSDAY

WORRIES	AND THEN WHAT?

FRIDAY

WORRIES	AND THEN WHAT?

SATURDAY

WORRIES	AND THEN WHAT?

XVI.   WEEK EIGHT - JUDGING

Be curious, not judgmental.
Walt Whitman

Most of us tend to judge everyone and everything, and although this may seem awful, some judgment is actually a necessary skill, and because of our old DNA, it is second nature for us. We need to know who can be trusted and who can't but critically judging ourselves and others constantly wears on us and we can make ourselves feel terrible, so it needs to be controlled.

JUDGING OTHERS

We started out judging others to understand who could be trusted, which was crucial for living in primitive conditions. Today, ascertaining who is unstable and needs monitoring for public safety remains vital to our survival, and we must be aware of our surroundings and those in our vicinity. It is important to know where the exits are and who seems out of control when we are in a new location with lots of people around. But we no longer notice this. Instead, our modern brain judges people to see if they are cool, popular, or better than we are. We tend to compare ourselves to everyone around us and this is a huge roadblock to getting a grip.

Envy is an ugly, devastating thought process. We can look at someone who is fit and easily think how lucky they are to be born that way. We might even grumble and wish we had their body. This thought ends up making us feel grumpy and resentful. Sound familiar? You might not resonate with the fit person example, but I would bet my bottom dollar you have compared yourself to someone else for any number of reasons and wished at some level you had what they have. That, my friend, is envy rearing its ugly head.

Before I did some fact checking I used to be envious of thin people. I believed thin people were somehow remarkably blessed and I was frustrated that I didn't have their good fortune. After doing some research, I learned the truth. People who are in shape manage closely what they do and what they eat.

Whatever the reason is for making comparisons, when we don't challenge our beliefs, we can get caught up in thoughts that aren't even true and allow them to derail our day. To GET A GRIP, this needs to change. All of us need to learn each and every one of us is grappling with something, and none of us is better than another. To help me remember, I use the mantra – be as kind as possible, everyone is battling something.

Old DNA has us constantly feeling "less than". As kids humans are experts at comparing themselves to others and thinking thoughts that make them feel worried, scared, mad or sad. Young people quickly learn to think friends have left them, the whispers are about them, and no one likes them.

JUDGING OURSELVES

We all carry around a vague idea of how we think we "should" be, and this is based on the image of what we consider perfect, something we made up in our head. To add more damage to what we do to ourselves just by what we think, we don't clearly define this image of what is perfect even though it has a huge impact on our satisfaction. Whatever "should be" we create, we hold it up as a trophy to win. And our "should be" is usually some random, vague, unrealistic goal. We create it, want to attain it, and all day compare where we are with where we "should be" and make ourselves feel like we will never measure up.

Do you remember that kid saying, nobody likes me, everybody hates me, I think I'll go eat worms? It's a kids' song because it shows how kids feel. Left unattended, as we age, our nobody likes me and our "should be" thoughts remain with us.

Our "should be" often centers on what we think makes us worthy of friendship and/or recognition, but instead of feeling worthy, it makes us feel like we are anything but that.

I learned to illustrate this point from a wonderful counselor. He said we all seem to have an idea roaming around in our head of what it would mean to be perfect, or to "have made it". And we believe if we arrive there everyone will see us as magnificent.

Yet we don't really define this idea or this idea is so outrageous we make ourselves worn out trying to achieve it. And as you know, all this happens without us really knowing it is.

For the illustration, which helps us put into perspective our thought process surrounding this idea, imagine a blank piece of paper placed landscape (rather than portrait) in front of you.

Your "should be" is a scribble in the upper right-hand corner. (It is a scribble because it is undefined) This is who you think you are supposed to be in order to be judged as worthy or ideal.

For where you are, go to the bottom left corner. Draw another scribble there and let it represent you at this moment in time. Connect the scribbles with lines and let them represent you checking in all day long to see if you have arrived at your "should be". All day we check, are we there? And since we aren't we feel miserable. But where are we actually headed?

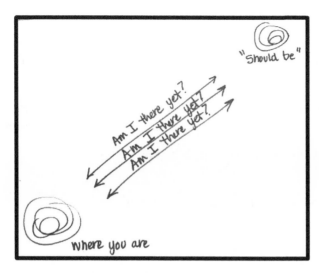

Instead of having a random, vague, and unrealistic "should be" it is healthier to set a specific, attainable goal close to where you are currently and work on achieving that.

Goals are best achieved when they are defined as smart goals. Writing goals according to specific outcomes (S), which are measurable (M), making sure what you want is actually attainable (A), setting realistic expectations as to how you will accomplish your goal (R) and how long it will take (T) is what it means to set S.M.A.R.T. goals. When we do the work to define what we truly want, we have taken a step toward changing our "should be" to "can be".

Example

I want to learn to speak Spanish.

(S) I want to be able to order food at a restaurant by speaking Spanish.

(M) I will be able to order a basic meal in Spanish

(A) I will learn to read, write and speak 25 words per week.

(R) My realistic path is to study 30 minutes per day.

(T) My goal will take 25 weeks to complete.

Counter example – I want to speak basic conversational Spanish in three weeks. Although this is Specific and measurable it is not attainable nor realistic and does not provide enough time to complete.

YOUR SMART GOAL	Date Started
S – write down a very specific goal you want to attain	
M – how will you measure that you reached your goal	
A – is what you want actually attainable?	
R – realistic path to accomplish your goal	
T – time required to reach your goal	

AS YOU JUDGE YOU ERODE YOUR JOY

Once you catch yourself having "should be" thoughts, it will become second nature not to think them. Have no fear, you are not alone on this journey. We all share the human experience, and, because of that, we share common "shoulds" and worries.

Our common worries are:

- · What do other people think of us
- · Are we perfect
- · We don't have any control or power
- · Things are scarce
- · Fear of failure
- · Need for certainty

· Comparing ourselves to others

· Our self-worth

· We are always anxious

· Self-doubt and "shoulds"

· Being calm, cool, and popular

All these can fill our mind with negative thoughts and create feelings of unworthiness. In order to GET A GRIP, we need to be aware that what we think on a regular basis has more influence on our emotions than we can imagine.

Just knowing this list of worries helps us better recognize what we are thinking and bring it to the forefront of our mind. We must remind ourselves that we were born with promise and potential and we can change what we think about.

You might have similar messages running around in your head. I overcame the judging others and myself obstacle by checking in with my thoughts, learning to hear what I am telling myself, and stopping the barrage of negativity by clarifying the definition of what it means to be or do something.

You can too.

You can change a message of "You are too loud" by asking in what way, or what decibel level deems one as too loud.

You can change a message of "You are wrong" by telling yourself I can't know everything, no one does, and failure is part of any process of learning.

You can change a message of "You must succeed" by answering for yourself what it means to be successful.

Life is often chaotic. You know it, and I know it. And when things are out of control, we tend to judge ourselves and others. You might think it is crazy to talk about having order when we should be talking about how to overcome judgment but order and good thinking habits go hand in hand.

Let me give you some examples of why order is important. Think about the items you use daily. They are in a special location, all with good reason, so that we can locate them with ease. Have you ever thought about why we have a designated drawer for eating utensils and it is always the same one? Can you imagine if you changed this location every time you did the dishes? Do you know how frustrated you would be when you try to find a fork for your salad? Or have you ever wondered why we have an underwear or sock drawer? Can you imagine how hard it would be to get dressed if that changed each day? Order staves off frustration.

The biggest bonus of being orderly, organized, cleaned up, ready to go, etc., is it makes completing tasks that much more likely, and excuses a thing of the past, which makes all of us feel accomplished with no need to judge. When we are organized, we aren't caught off guard, we know what is coming, and we have what we need when we need it. We don't feel the need to judge ourselves as idiots for forgetting something.

When we are organized and orderly, not only are our drawers in order, so is our sense of preparedness. And when we are organized and remain orderly in what, when and how we run our lives, we feel a sense of "I've got this", and with that feeling running in our veins we have less need for judgmental thoughts.

System - To Get A Grip we must stop judging. This might be the hardest task of all. If you have built this habit, you can, with work, break it. To change your pattern of judging start small and practice not judging or criticizing anyone or anything for one hour.

For one hour, try to think only positive thoughts about people you don't know. Once you have accomplished this small segment of time, move on to longer stretches until you can reach a full day with only nonjudgmental thoughts of others.

Then move on to work on not judging people you do know. again, start small and move on to longer stretches of time.

Finally, remain neutral about anyone or anything for 10 days to develop a new, better habit.

Then move on to you. Really focus on the disparaging remarks you make about yourself. You know, the ones you say in an attempt to be humble or help others not feel badly about themselves, but which in reality just make you feel bad. Or the things you say to yourself when you miss an appointment or make a mistake.

When you are late for an appointment or you have made a mistake, what is the first thing you say to yourself? I would lay money on the fact that you start complaining about how you are so dumb and can't do anything right. Or you worry and fret about the excuse you will use for being late. Forget about making excuses and worrying about what others will think. Instead, say to yourself, "You've got this" and move on.

To motivate yourself to meet this goal, try paying a dollar into a jar every time you think something negative, even something small, about yourself or others. A dollar is a large enough sum to motivate a change. It won't take long to feel the pinch and stop. If you want additional motivation, you can use the money to help a worthy organization help others. This in turn helps you too.

Routine – set a routine to maintain order in your thoughts and avoid judgment by remembering to validate your thinking with "Is that true?"

Small first step – to be organized and stave off feeling out of control which leads to judgement of yourself, start to implement order in where things are. You can start small – perhaps the toiletry items you use each morning. Think of ways that will work to have them in order, ready to go.

Then, when you have mastered a few small things, you can move on to bigger ticket items. If you have a friend who is good at organizing, enlist their help; doing it together will make it more fun.

TRACKING PROGRESS - WEEK EIGHT

JUDGING OURSELVES AND OTHERS							
START YOUR DAYS WITH INTENTION CENTERED ON SELF-CARE. THINK ZERO NEGATIVE THOUGHTS ABOUT HOW YOU ARE, WHO OTHERS ARE, WHAT YOU OR THEY ARE DOING.							
	SUN	MON	TUES	WED	THUR	FRI	SAT
MAKE YOUR BED							
GRATITUDE/JOY JOURNAL							
JUDGING OURSELVES AND OTHERS							

Sunday through Saturday

Each time you judge yourself or others, ask yourself for proof of your thoughts, and make sure you know of what you speak.

To motivate real change, you can charge yourself one dollar for each time you judge yourself or others. Get immediate feedback by giving that dollar to someone around you so that you feel the impact of judgment. In this way, you can train yourself to stop being judgmental and free your thoughts to be more positive.

JOURNAL PAGE

13 WEEK SCHEDULE -WEEK EIGHT

JUDGING OURSELVES AND OTHERS							
START YOUR DAYS WITH INTENTION CENTERED ON SELF-CARE. THINK ZERO NEGATIVE THOUGHTS ABOUT HOW YOU ARE, WHO OTHERS ARE, WHAT YOU OR THEY ARE DOING.							
	SUN	MON	TUES	WED	THUR	FRI	SAT
MAKE YOUR BED							
GRATITUDE/JOY JOURNAL							
JUDGING OURSELVES AND OTHERS							

GRATITUDES   JOY

MONDAY

GRATITUDES	JOY
1.	1.
2.	2.
3.	3.
4.	4.
5.	5.

TUESDAY

1.	1.
2.	2.
3.	3.
4.	4.
5.	5.

WEDNESDAY

1.	1.
2.	2.
3.	3.
4.	4.
5.	5.

THURSDAY

1.	1.
2.	2.
3.	3.
4.	4.
5.	5.

GRATITUDES   JOY

FRIDAY

GRATITUDES	JOY
1.	1.
2.	2.
3.	3.
4.	4.
5.	5.

SATURDAY

1.	1.
2.	2.
3.	3.
4.	4.
5.	5.

SUNDAY

1.	1.
2.	2.
3.	3.
4.	4.
5.	5.

MORE IN DEPTH TRACKING
SUNDAY THROUGH SATURDAY

JUDGING OURSELVES AND OTHERS							
START YOUR DAYS WITH INTENTION CENTERED ON SELF-CARE. THINK ZERO NEGATIVE THOUGHTS ABOUT HOW YOU ARE, WHO OTHERS ARE, WHAT YOU OR THEY ARE DOING.							
	SUN	MON	TUES	WED	THUR	FRI	SAT
MAKE YOUR BED							
GRATITUDE/JOY JOURNAL							
JUDGING OURSELVES AND OTHERS							

Each time you judge yourself or others, ask yourself for proof of your thoughts, and make sure you know of what you speak. And keep a tally of each time. As you work on your goals this week check off each item as it is completed each day.

SUNDAY

MAKE YOUR BED	
MORNING ROUTINE	
ORGANIZE YOUR BELONGINGS	
SELF JUDGMENT	
JUDGMENT OF OTHERS	
EVENING ROUTINE	

MONDAY

MAKE YOUR BED	
MORNING ROUTINE	
ORGANIZE YOUR BELONGINGS	
SELF JUDGMENT	
JUDGMENT OF OTHERS	
EVENING ROUTINE	

TUESDAY

MAKE YOUR BED	
MORNING ROUTINE	
ORGANIZE YOUR BELONGING	
SELF JUDGMENT	
JUDGMENT OF OTHERS	
EVENING ROUTINE	

WEDNESDAY

MAKE YOUR BED	
MORNING ROUTINE	
ORGANIZE YOUR BELONGING	
SELF JUDGMENT	
JUDGMENT OF OTHERS	
EVENING ROUTINE	

THURSDAY

MAKE YOUR BED	
MORNING ROUTINE	
ORGANIZE YOUR BELONGING	
SELF JUDGMENT	
JUDGMENT OF OTHERS	
EVENING ROUTINE	

FRIDAY

MAKE YOUR BED	
MORNING ROUTINE	
ORGANIZE YOUR BELONGING	
SELF JUDGMENT	
JUDGMENT OF OTHERS	
EVENING ROUTINE	

SATURDAY

MAKE YOUR BED	
MORNING ROUTINE	
ORGANIZE YOUR BELONGING	
SELF JUDGMENT	
JUDGMENT OF OTHERS	
EVENING ROUTINE	

XVII.　WEEK NINE - AM I?

To be happy, we must not be too concerned with others.
Albert Camus

I spent many years needlessly worrying about what other people thought of me and my work rather than focusing on my own expectations. Of course, I didn't even realize I was doing so. Thankfully, I learned a great strategy that helped me overcome this focus on what others think. I learned this from a colleague of mine who was a school counselor. He helped me center my thoughts on what I think is important, rather than giving others my power.

FOCUS ON YOU

To center my thoughts on what I think, he told me to ask myself Am I questions. Examples of these are:

> Am I happy with how I look?
> Am I satisfied with the work I produce?

Am I...?

Now whenever a worry about what I am doing, how I look, or the work I am producing arises I remind myself I have the power to decide when, how and what I do, and it matters what I think. I can't control the thoughts of others or know what they are thinking.

I check my mind often by asking my "Am I..." questions and I do this each time I think negative thoughts about me. I practice consistently to create a better thought habit.

I set goals that have meaning to me and work toward being the best person I want to be.

You can use focus questions too. So, can your loved ones.

Ask yourself:

> Am I happy/satisfied with what I am doing?
> Is this my best work?
> Am I proud of what I've accomplished?

If the answer is no, reflect on improvements for future endeavors, but don't berate yourself. Making yourself feel badly and unworthy will not improve who you are or what you do.

As the saying goes – "You do You". No one makes you feel happy, sad, mad, etc. You do. You and only you oversee your emotions. Therefore, learning to focus on you is a very important step to getting a grip.

Center your thoughts on what YOU think, return your power to you. Ask yourself "Am I" questions to align your actions with your goals for yourself.

YOUR CHOICES – YOUR RESPONSIBILITY

Remind yourself you have the power to decide when, how and what you do, because you are the one who will have to answer for each choice you make, and it matters what you think

You can help your loved one understand emotions work this way and teaching them focus questions, and how thoughts work, especially negative ones, will help them in their lives, which will enable them to reach their promise and potential.

TRACKING PROGRESS – WEEK NINE

AM I ...?							
MEET YOUR OWN EXPECTATIONS AND ASK "AM I... HAPPY WITH WHAT I AM DOING, WEARING, SAYING, ETC."							
	SUN	MON	TUES	WED	THUR	FRI	SAT
MAKE YOUR BED							
GRATITUDE/JOY JOURNAL							
AM I?							

Sunday through Saturday

Each day focus on your decisions and actions and note if they are in line with your goals for yourself, or are you doing what you imagine others desire from you?

Are you pleasing yourself?

Are you exercising self-care?

Are you setting goals and doing your best work?

Or are you a people pleaser first and putting yourself last?

JOURNAL PAGE

13 WEEK SCHEDULE -WEEK NINE

AM I ...?							
MEET YOUR OWN EXPECTATIONS AND ASK "AM I... HAPPY WITH WHAT I AM DOING, WEARING, SAYING, ETC."							
	SUN	MON	TUES	WED	THUR	FRI	SAT
MAKE YOUR BED							
GRATITUDE/JOY JOURNAL							
AM I?							

GRATITUDES   JOY
MONDAY
1.   1.
2.   2.
3.   3.
4.   4.
5.   5.

TUESDAY
1.   1.
2.   2.
3.   3.
4.   4.
5.   5.

WEDNESDAY
1.   1.
2.   2.
3.   3.
4.   4.
5.   5.

THURSDAY
1.   1.
2.   2.
3.   3.
4.   4.
5.   5.

GRATITUDES   JOY
FRIDAY
1.   1.
2.   2.
3.   3.
4.   4.
5.   5.

SATURDAY
1.   1.
2.   2.
3.   3.
4.   4.
5.   5.

SUNDAY
1.   1.
2.   2.
3.   3.
4.   4.
5.   5.

MORE IN DEPTH TRACKING
SUNDAY THROUGH SATURDAY

AM I ...?							
MEET YOUR OWN EXPECTATIONS AND ASK "AM I... HAPPY WITH WHAT I AM DOING, WEARING, SAYING, ETC."							
	SUN	MON	TUES	WED	THUR	FRI	SAT
MAKE YOUR BED							
GRATITUDE/JOY JOURNAL							
AM I?							

Each day focus on your decisions and actions and note if they are in line with what you want for yourself. When we make decisions, we can base them on those around us rather than what brings us joy. And when we focus too much on what others want rather than speaking our wants and needs, we can get worn out and lose our grip.

Sunday

Time	Decision	Why did you decide this?

Monday

Time	Decision	Why did you decide this?

Tuesday

Time	Decision	Why did you decide this?

Wednesday

Time	Decision	Why did you decide this?

Thursday

Time	Decision	Why did you decide this?

Friday

Time	Decision	Why did you decide this?

Saturday

Time	Decision	Why did you decide this?

XVIII. WEEK TEN - TRIGGERS

Speak when you are angry and you will
make the best speech you will ever
regret.
Ambrose Bierce

Have you ever lost your cool and didn't understand why? We all have. This happens when we are caught off guard by what someone says or does, or by how we perceive we are treated. When this happens, we tend to respond in a way we didn't choose. When we feel something intensely – when it triggers us - we usually have an out-of-control reaction.

175

Each time you react in a big way, whether silently or aloud, pay attention, this is your body telling you what needs attention.

TRIGGERS SET US OFF

When you have a raw tickle in your throat what is your first thought? Sore throat, right? Every adult knows what it means to have a sore throat. We have all experienced one and through the years have learned to recognize one early. When you feel a sore throat coming on, you first try to ignore it, hoping it is all in your head. True? But once you accept defeat and you know for sure that this is indeed a sore throat, you know what to do because you have been taught. You ramp into high gear and start using all the remedies you have learned and developed. We all like to share our remedies. No one misses a chance to tell someone else what works for them, and how their cocktail cure is the best, sure to fix whatever ails the people around them. (My go to is zinc lozenges, just fyi). Once the cold arrives you recognize that too, and have learned what to do to minimize the effects, correct?

But when it comes to emotions, the opposite is true. Whenever someone is emotional and could really use some advice, it is as if they are in a library. No one around them makes a sound. No one is willing to explain how they have suffered depression, been too scared to try, or tell of the times they have been so angry they said and did some awful things. No one wants to admit the intimate details of when they screamed at the top of their lungs at their spouse, spanked their kids, or when they were so sad, they spent the day in bed sobbing, unable to ask for help from others. Instead of offering or asking for support, we all clam up and keep our troubles to ourselves.

Wouldn't it be great if we didn't clam up? If we shared the telltale signs of our emotions so that others could learn to recognize what they are feeling and what worked for us? Think of how comforting that would be.

But this is not how we as a society have handled emotional intelligence. It seems when one of us learns something that works, something that helps them handle their emotions, they don't want to teach the rest of us how to recognize emotions or options of how to deal with them. We don't talk to each other about the many different emotions that exist or where to recognize them in our body, which is an important topic because that is where the emotions first arise. These discussions are exactly what we need to do to help all of us GET A GRIP and rise above being triggered by experiences in our lives that cause us to explode with emotion.

EXPLOSION OF EMOTION

These explosions are one of the biggest barriers to getting a grip and they happen in the blink of an eye as we are blindsided by our emotional responses. We get triggered by some thought that pops into our head which creates such an intense feeling that we burst open with emotion. And the emotions created from our thoughts get the best of us and make us do and say what we don't intend. Big emotions often push us to a place where we don't want to be, sorry for our words and or actions. If you have ever snapped at a loved one, you know this and understand all too well what I am saying. We get triggered and respond before we can GET A GRIP.

When we get triggered, it is our body and mind telling us "this" needs attention. When we feel something intensely – when it triggers us - that is when we need to really pay attention, because our emotions are telling us what needs work. Hidden behind our response are the deep-seated thoughts and beliefs that need to come to the surface and be changed.

I see this all the time. Let me give you an example of a young student who ended up in my office when I was an Elementary Administrator after being triggered and shouting out the F word at his friend. I was so surprised to meet with him on a disciplinary action because he had never been in any sort of trouble before.

When I learned it was for swearing my surprise vanished because he was in fourth grade, a typical age for swearing to happen.

Let me set the stage a bit and connect the experience to triggers. Being in the principal's office has the same effect on young and old. No one wants to be there, even grown up, out of school, parents. Everyone feels guilty and scared and, knowing this, I always made sure to set a welcoming tone and environment.

I knew this young man was "freaked out" so I started by reassuring him I still thought of him as a nice young man and it was what he did that wasn't great. (Often, unintentionally, we communicate that the child is bad when they need discipline, and it is important to make the distinction between what they do and who they are. When reprimanding any child, always explain, I love you, I just don't like what you did.) I tried to tell him everything was going to be okay, but he was hearing none of it, he knew his mother would react with disappointment. He didn't think about the impact on his mum when he blurted out the infamous F word, but he for sure knew it in my office.

We talked through the series of events that led up to the interaction. His friend had ignored him in line, and he assumed his buddy didn't want to be his friend anymore. So, he said, "F you." Can you recognize his limiting belief? He feels unworthy and doesn't realize this is what he is thinking.

After our discussion, he was able to realize his feelings that arose from assuming he was not liked by his friend, and they led him down his path of no return until they made him want to hurt his friend. To overcome his trigger, he needed to learn not to assume what others are thinking. Rather, he should ask the other person what they are thinking in order to be clearer about someone's intentions. This knowledge can help him GET A GRIP and avoid a similar trigger in the future.

When allowed to run wild and uncontrolled, our "big feelings" reach a point of no return and we get triggered. And when we are triggered, we usually have an out-of-control reaction. We often take out our frustration, anger, disappointment, hurt, etc. on those we love most and then feel embarrassment and shame. We want to hurt the people who made us mad, but instead we take it out on our loved ones because we know they will forgive us.

But should we? Do they deserve this? Can't we do better?

Children are very susceptible to this. Have you ever heard a child tell their parents, "I hate you!" They take out their frustration on those they love. Children also tend to say something hurtful to their classmates and friends because they haven't developed their interpersonal skills yet. Due to the fact that they want to hide their mistakes, they don't want to admit they were wrong, they struggle to apologize, so instead they blurt out "I hate you, you aren't my friend." Or even worse, F you.

Being triggered drives us into dangerous territory because sometimes the words and actions we let out do so much damage we can't salvage the relationship. And like nails hammered into a fence, even when they are removed, they leave a permanent mark. This is not what we intend, but it can be the impact of what we say and do.

Perhaps when you get triggered you scream and yell and maybe swear which gets you nowhere and only makes you look like a two-year-old having a tantrum.

Or maybe when you are triggered you don't yell or scream but rather you are silent but still feel enormous turmoil inside.

Neither of these responses allows you to get what you need because to communicate what you desire you must remain cool, calm, and collected. Everyone deserves to be heard and understood but that is only possible if we can state our needs and concerns in a way that others can understand.

The remedy to use when triggers happen is to stop immediately before you say or do anything, and then use a breathing technique to calm yourself. Finally, be still long enough to hear what you are thinking. Recall the fact that thoughts create feelings which then turn into actions. So, when you are triggered to act in a way you don't want, you need to return to the thoughts that caused the action so you can change them and respond to life's situations in a way you desire.

By recognizing what you are feeling and then having a planned response, you can gain control to choose how you want to respond rather than allowing life to control you. The problem is that when we are triggered it all happens so quickly, and because we don't stop right then and there and listen for the root cause of our thinking, we don't realize what occurred in the beginning, or why.

To avoid all of that upset, we can prevent the explosion by analyzing what triggers us. Just like my former student who didn't realize he was so hurt and all he wanted to feel was the power of his anger, you, too, can learn your trigger points to avoid reactions you don't choose.

One such trigger trap happens to me when I am looking for validation as a talented, good, smart, pretty, capable, loving, kind, awesome human. (Not too much to ask, right?) This is the classic worthy trigger trap. When I am tired this is usually what my thoughts are thinking. Knowing I can get this way and, in order to be prepared for activities that take me outside my comfort zone which cause me to doubt myself and my abilities, I have to plan ahead for the emotions that will be created. When I plan that big emotions will be triggered, I can recognize them early and avoid actions I don't choose.

Now, I may sound like I have my life all in order, but trust me, I am a work in progress. Even with all the work I do I still get triggered by the same things over and over again but planning ahead helps me avoid outbursts. And my recovery time is much less.

If you take time to Stop, Breathe, and Listen, you will be able to not only understand what set you off, but also be able to choose the response you want to have.

BREATHE

To handle our big feelings with the grace we desire we can learn the simple act of breathing, which calms us every time. When you start to feel emotions building, stop, and breathe. Breathe deeply, slowly in, and slowly out. Count to 4 slowly while breathing in, hold your breath for 4 counts, and then while counting four more, let your breath out. Concentrate on slowing your heart rate and only focus on your breathing. Once you can do four counts, the next goal is to do it for 8. Normally, we find ourselves needing to do this while in the company of others, so when that happens, breathe as deeply as you can without being obvious. I use this technique to calm myself when flying and it works beautifully for that, too.

Concentrating on your breathing gives your brain time to think and catch up to your emotions. If you can force yourself to deep breathe before you let out your feelings, you will be amazed at the amount of grace you have to handle the trials and tribulations of your life.

When we plan ahead and have things in order, when we have taken time for ourselves and are rested and well, we can maintain our sense of self, stave off the chaos of life, know what lies ahead, and be prepared mentally and emotionally to take on any challenge.

When we start each day on the "right" foot, by having things ready to go we create a sense of control. A former colleague of mine laid out her clothes and jewelry for the week each Sunday. She was impeccably dressed and planned for special days such as holidays, etc. She chose her jewelry, clothes, and shoes to create the biggest impact and to communicate her confidence and commitment to the company. Even though I love to wear the perfect ensemble, I have never been able to accomplish choosing work clothes in advance of wearing them, but I do just that when planning to work out. I have gym gear organized, in the same location, which ensures I go. I also pack early for a trip, and repack several times, so that I have what I will need. And I use a backpack for everything work related, because having necessary items in their set place ensures I have what I need and don't need to scramble or worry.

When we are organized, not only do we avoid judgement, worry and fear, we are better able to create a sense of calm and can avoid being triggered. Sundays are a perfect day to plan for the week ahead.

If you have a family, have your "team" meeting on this day. I am a fan of these meetings because they are great for catching up on how everyone is doing, allow everyone to feel heard, and are an opportunity to lay out the plan for the week. The use of a calendar to plan for activities, homework, tests, sporting events and the like helps everyone gain a sense of autonomy and confidence.

As the team plans for the week, look at which days will be stressful, which days will demand your best, and how you will support one another when need be.

Triggers are best avoided when we know what is coming and are prepared for the big emotions that will arise.

System – Each time you feel a big emotion, it means you have been triggered. Immediately STOP whatever you are doing or saying and push the pause button. Sit with the feeling and let it work through you. Know you are feeling it, but don't allow yourself to interact. Just feel but don't respond. Think of the root thought that is causing the trigger. Learn to understand why you feel what you feel, and always remember much of what you think is just what you make up in your head. Take the time to prove your faulty thinking wrong.

Routine – When you start to feel emotions building, stop, and breathe. Breathe deeply, slowly in, and slowly out. Count to 4 slowly while breathing in, hold your breath for 4 counts, and then while counting four more, let your breath out. Concentrate on slowing your heart rate and only focus on your breathing. Once you can easily do four counts, move on to 8

Small first step – The process to overcome being triggered isn't an easy one. It will take practice. Over time, you will master what sets you off and learn to think different thoughts. But for now, start with the small first step of breathing.

TRACKING PROGRESS - WEEK TEN

TRIGGERS - BREATHE							
GET TO THE BASIS OF WHAT SETS YOU OFF SO THAT YOU CAN REMOVE THOSE NEGATIVE THOUGHTS AND BELIEFS ONCE AND FOR ALL. LEARN TO STOP AND BREATHE.							
	SUN	MON	TUES	WED	THUR	FRI	SAT
MAKE YOUR BED							
GRATITUDE/JOY JOURNAL							
TRIGGERS - BREATHE							

Sunday through Saturday

Each time you react in a big way, whether silently or aloud, note what triggered you. Stop immediately and really concentrate on the emotion coursing through your veins. Learn the basis for what you are feeling. These are your triggers.

When you start to feel emotions building, stop, and breathe. Breathe deeply, slowly in, and slowly out. Count to 4 slowly while breathing in, hold your breath for 4 counts, and then let your breath out for four counts. Concentrate on slowing your heart rate and only focus on your breathing. Once you can do four counts, the next goal is to do it for 8.

JOURNAL PAGE

13 WEEK SCHEDULE -WEEK TEN

TRIGGERS - BREATHE							
GET TO THE BASIS OF WHAT SETS YOU OFF SO THAT YOU CAN REMOVE THOSE NEGATIVE THOUGHTS AND BELIEFS ONCE AND FOR ALL. LEARN TO STOP AND BREATHE.							
	SUN	MON	TUES	WED	THUR	FRI	SAT
MAKE YOUR BED							
GRATITUDE/JOY JOURNAL							
TRIGGERS - BREATHE							

GRATITUDES   JOY

MONDAY
1.   1.
2.   2.
3.   3.
4.   4.
5.   5.

TUESDAY
1.   1.
2.   2.
3.   3.
4.   4.
5.   5.

WEDNESDAY
1.   1.
2.   2.
3.   3.
4.   4.
5.   5.

THURSDAY
1.   1.
2.   2.
3.   3.
4.   4.
5.   5.

GRATITUDES   JOY

FRIDAY
1.   1.
2.   2.
3.   3.
4.   4.
5.   5.

SATURDAY
1.   1.
2.   2.
3.   3.
4.   4.
5.   5.

SUNDAY
1.   1.
2.   2.
3.   3.
4.   4.
5.   5.

MORE IN DEPTH TRACKING
SUNDAY THROUGH SATURDAY

TRIGGERS - BREATHE							
GET TO THE BASIS OF WHAT SETS YOU OFF SO THAT YOU CAN REMOVE THOSE NEGATIVE THOUGHTS AND BELIEFS ONCE AND FOR ALL. LEARN TO STOP AND BREATHE.							
	SUN	MON	TUES	WED	THUR	FRI	SAT
MAKE YOUR BED							
GRATITUDE/JOY JOURNAL							
TRIGGERS - BREATHE							

Keep track of what triggers you so that you can analyze and defuse your trigger points. They won't go away entirely but you can learn to manage them and make your recovery time much shorter.

SUNDAY

EMOTION FELT	TRIGGER RESPONSE

MONDAY

EMOTION FELT	TRIGGER RESPONSE

TUESDAY

EMOTION FELT	TRIGGER RESPONSE

WEDNESDAY

EMOTION FELT	TRIGGER RESPONSE

THURSDAY

EMOTION FELT	TRIGGER RESPONSE

FRIDAY

EMOTION FELT	TRIGGER RESPONSE

SATURDAY

EMOTION FELT	TRIGGER RESPONSE

XIX. WEEK ELEVEN - PLANNING AHEAD

If you fail to plan, you are planning to fail!
Benjamin Franklin

We get overwhelmed when we are unprepared and outside our comfort/control zone. When we plan for the different emotions we might experience in a given activity or place, we are better able to maintain our grip.

When we know we are headed into an activity that triggers our emotional state of mind, we need to develop a plan ahead of time, look at our schedule and know what is headed our way.

PLAN YOUR RESPONSES

Because each day brings new experiences that demand our best, I can't stress enough the importance of planning ahead and developing strategies to handle your emotions before an issue arises.

When you prepare, you can react in the way you desire rather than have an outburst that goes completely wrong. Instead of stuffing feelings and keeping emotions inside which causes an emotional explosion based on an old hurt or bad memory, you can get to the root cause of your pain points and be ready with your chosen response.

As I was being raised, feelings weren't discussed. Nor were we allowed to feel. Left to decipher emotions on my own I learned to recognize and use the three biggies: mad, sad, glad. To be honest, they were mostly mad and sad. This is a very limited list of emotions and certainly not extensive enough to GET A GRIP.

When we plan for the different emotions we might experience in a given activity or place, we are more likely to be able to maintain our grip. Focusing on our weekly schedule helps us do just that as does taking time for rest and relaxation and doing things we enjoy.

Like we do with a sore throat, to avoid being triggered, we must learn to recognize what we are feeling. Sadly, this isn't something we are normally taught to do, but it is something we can learn. No one and no item can make you feel and react. You do that by how you control your thoughts. And you can feel and react the way you choose when you prepare for what is coming your way not just with schedule but with specific emotional responses too.

To GET A GRIP, we can teach ourselves (and our loved ones) to recognize many emotions and develop reactions to each that are best for us. For example, think of a time when you were sad, how did you respond? Did it work well? What else could you do?

And what about when you are disappointed with yourself? With others? What do you do then?

I make sure I let my nearest and dearest know if I am sad or disappointed so they know I need help and that it isn't about them (unless it is).

When you are mad, how do you react? Is that the appropriate response? What other responses could you have? Do you understand what made you mad? Do you understand anger is most often a response to your hurt feelings and it makes you feel like you need your power restored?

As I told you earlier, mad is one of my go to emotions. I have learned to change that by implementing strategies such as doing relaxation breathing and if possible, soaking in a hot bath. Often just washing my face with cold water, or my hands work too, will change my physical response and snap me back to thinking more clearly.

There are many feelings and many possible responses. Feelings and emotions aren't necessarily bad. They help us relate to ourselves and others and they alert us to what needs attention. It is when the feelings and emotions take control of our lives, and cause us to react in ways we don't like, that we need to remember the fact that thoughts create feelings and those feelings create actions. We GET A GRIP by learning to control what we think so that our feelings and actions are what we want.

LOOK AHEAD

Being disciplined about where I allow my brain to wander is mandatory to "gripping" a life of abundance, gratitude, and happiness. Isn't that what we all want, to GET A GRIP and live a full happy life?

Being happy isn't based on a new car, a new house, a new outfit, etc., it doesn't work that way. Our mental state is what manages our emotions and it is our responsibility to make ourselves happy. No one and no item can make us happy. We do that by controlling our thoughts. And controlling our thoughts means we can control our actions.

When we know we are headed into an activity that triggers our emotional state of mind, we need to develop a plan ahead of time. We need to ready ourselves emotionally to not fall into our own trigger traps.

WHERE DO YOU FEEL YOUR EMOTIONS?

The first place we feel an emotion is in our body. To be better able to respond well, we need to know where we feel our emotions first because this helps us recognize when triggers are forming.

Using the sketch below choose colors to represent some of the common emotions of anger, love, happiness, and fear and overlay them on the body where you feel them.

For example, love might be represented by red and felt in your arms and lips. Why? Because hugs and kisses go along with love.

Anger may be black and might give you a pain in your stomach or tension in your back.

Sad might be gray and be felt in your chest.

Now add where you feel emotions in your body to your plan for how you can react to the following emotions:

STRESSED	
Where you feel this emotion in your body -	
Possible good responses	

DISAPPOINTED	
Where you feel this emotion in your body -	
Possible good responses	

DISGUSTED	
Where you feel this emotion in your body -	
Possible good responses	

EMBARRASSED	
Where you feel this emotion in your body -	
Possible good responses	

HAPPY	
Where you feel this emotion in your body -	
Possible good responses	

MAD	
Where you feel this emotion in your body -	
Possible good responses	

OVERWHELMED	
Where you feel this emotion in your body -	
Possible good responses	

SAD	
Where you feel this emotion in your body -	
Possible good responses	

SURPRIZED	
Where you feel this emotion in your body -	
Possible good responses	

YOUR FEELINGS HAVE BEEN HURT	
Where you feel this emotion in your body -	
Possible good responses	

AFRAID	
Where you feel this emotion in your body -	
Possible good responses	

You can add other emotions to your list and be prepared for those too.

TRACKING PROGRESS - WEEK ELEVEN

PLAN AHEAD							
THINK AHEAD TO WHAT YOUR SCHEDULE HAS IN STORE, SPECIFICALLY THOSE EXPERIENCES THAT WILL CREATE BIG EMOTIONS. AND THEN PLAN HOW YOU WILL RESPOND BEFORE IT ALL HAPPENS.							
	SUN	MON	TUES	WED	THUR	FRI	SAT
MAKE YOUR BED							
GRATITUDE/JOY JOURNAL							
PLAN AHEAD							

Sunday through Saturday

Take time this week to set a schedule that works for you. Make sure to check and see if what you agree to do and what you say yes to is actually just you trying to belong which zaps your energy and joy.

Pay close attention to where and how you spend your time. Often, we spend time doing things we don't enjoy and forget to take care of ourselves. Plan times for self-care and rejuvenation.

Look for days and times in your schedule which will trigger your emotions. Use your list of possible reactions to emotions especially when you know you will be triggered. Pay attention to how you feel physically because triggered emotions are first felt in our body.

JOURNAL PAGE

13 WEEK SCHEDULE -WEEK ELEVEN

PLAN AHEAD							
THINK AHEAD TO WHAT YOUR SCHEDULE HAS IN STORE, SPECIFICALLY THOSE EXPERIENCES THAT WILL CREATE BIG EMOTIONS. AND THEN PLAN HOW YOU WILL RESPOND BEFORE IT ALL HAPPENS.							
	SUN	MON	TUES	WED	THUR	FRI	SAT
MAKE YOUR BED							
GRATITUDE/JOY JOURNAL							
PLAN AHEAD							

GRATITUDES　　JOY

MONDAY
1.　　　　　　1.
2.　　　　　　2.
3.　　　　　　3.
4.　　　　　　4.
5.　　　　　　5.

TUESDAY
1.　　　　　　1.
2.　　　　　　2.
3.　　　　　　3.
4.　　　　　　4.
5.　　　　　　5.

WEDNESDAY
1.　　　　　　1.
2.　　　　　　2.
3.　　　　　　3.
4.　　　　　　4.
5.　　　　　　5.

THURSDAY
1.　　　　　　1.
2.　　　　　　2.
3.　　　　　　3.
4.　　　　　　4.
5.　　　　　　5.

GRATITUDES　　JOY

FRIDAY
1.　　　　　　1.
2.　　　　　　2.
3.　　　　　　3.
4.　　　　　　4.
5.　　　　　　5.

SATURDAY
1.　　　　　　1.
2.　　　　　　2.
3.　　　　　　3.
4.　　　　　　4.
5.　　　　　　5.

SUNDAY
1.　　　　　　1.
2.　　　　　　2.
3.　　　　　　3.
4.　　　　　　4.
5.　　　　　　5.

MORE IN DEPTH TRACKING
SUNDAY THROUGH SATURDAY

PLAN AHEAD							
THINK AHEAD TO WHAT YOUR SCHEDULE HAS IN STORE, SPECIFICALLY THOSE EXPERIENCES THAT WILL CREATE BIG EMOTIONS. AND THEN PLAN HOW YOU WILL RESPOND BEFORE IT ALL HAPPENS.							
	SUN	MON	TUES	WED	THUR	FRI	SAT
MAKE YOUR BED							
GRATITUDE/JOY JOURNAL							
PLAN AHEAD							

Set a schedule that works for you. Pay close attention to where and how you spend your time. Put into play a schedule that helps you stay focused on what is important and necessary. Note your emotions and responses.

SUNDAY

Time	Where	Emotions and Responses
7AM		
8AM		
9AM		
10AM		
11AM		
12PM		
1PM		
2PM		
3PM		
4PM		
5PM		
6PM		
7PM		
8PM		

MONDAY

Time	Where	Emotions and Responses
7AM		
8AM		
9AM		
10AM		
11AM		
12PM		
1PM		
2PM		
3PM		
4PM		
5PM		
6PM		
7PM		
8PM		

TUESDAY

Time	Where	Emotions and Responses
7AM		
8AM		
9AM		
10AM		
11AM		
12PM		
1PM		
2PM		
3PM		
4PM		
5PM		
6PM		
7PM		
8PM		

WEDNESDAY

Time	Where	Emotions and Responses
7AM		
8AM		
9AM		
10AM		
11AM		
12PM		
1PM		
2PM		
3PM		
4PM		
5PM		
6PM		
7PM		
8PM		

THURSDAY

Time	Where	Emotions and Responses
7AM		
8AM		
9AM		
10AM		
11AM		
12PM		
1PM		
2PM		
3PM		
4PM		
5PM		
6PM		
7PM		
8PM		

FRIDAY

Time	Where	Emotions and Responses
7AM		
8AM		
9AM		
10AM		
11AM		
12PM		
1PM		
2PM		
3PM		
4PM		
5PM		
6PM		
7PM		
8PM		

SATURDAY

Time	Where	Emotions and Responses
7AM		
8AM		
9AM		
10AM		
11AM		
12PM		
1PM		
2PM		
3PM		
4PM		
5PM		
6PM		
7PM		
8PM		

XX. WEEK TWELVE - THE CIRCLE OF TRUST

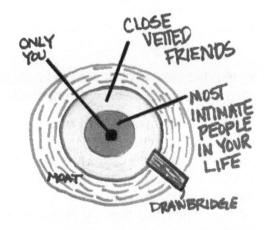

Most people have too many friends and do not enjoy an appropriately selected and reinforced inner circle.
Richard Koch - The 80/20 Principle

Most of our triggers occur when we are with other people. They do all sorts of things that tap into our emotions, they hurt our feelings, or they make a joke at our expense. Even if they don't mean to, they can ignite a response that sends us down the emotional path of no return. We can be left thinking that no one likes us, and we need to go eat worms.

That feeling can last too long.

To work on our triggers, let's focus on our interactions with people, because people can make us sad, disappointed, angry, irritated, embarrassed, you name it. This is especially true when dealing with friends. Because of our old DNA's need to belong to a safety group, we can accept people as friends and confidants too soon.

When we consider someone a friend and confidant, we allow them into what is known as our circle of trust. If you have ever seen the movie "Meet the Fockers", you will recall the dad's circle of trust.

Here is a clip of when the term was used
https://youtu.be/QHJGoZpFeM8

In this movie, the dad talks a lot about the family circle of trust and who belongs and how to be allowed entrance.

Building a circle of trust means we set boundaries for who belongs inside our inner circle, basically another way of saying our heart. A circle of trust works best when it contains only those we have vetted; those we can trust to have our back and ride into battle with us if need be. The problems that arise with our circle of trust stem from the fact we don't know how to set boundaries.

Often, we let people in our circle of trust only to realize they shouldn't be there because they did or said something that really hurt our feelings.

SET AND MAINTAIN BOUNDARIES

I first learned about setting relationship boundaries while working with Larry the Counselor. He taught me to view levels of close relationships as concentric circles.

The big idea being our "circle" of trust.

Think of this picture of concentric circles as a castle surrounded by a moat.

I use the castle example because it is important that we remember to always fortify and defend our heart, our circle of trust, and make sure no one can scale the walls and get inside without our permission.

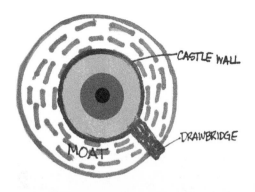

Imagine your circle of trust as three concentric circles. And further imagine these concentric circles as areas inside fortified castle walls. The castle is the area inside the black ring which represents the castle wall.

Inside the black ring you see light gray, dark gray, and black circles. Together these three concentric circles are what is considered your guarded circle of trust. Each area is reserved for specific levels of intimacy and requirements for who is allowed in.

The moat surrounds the castle to defend it from intruders. There is a drawbridge which crosses the moat that allows access to the castle. The drawbridge is lowered when you want to let people in otherwise it is up.

As you move toward the center circle each area is more exclusive.

The first light gray area is for your close vetted friends. They have your back, keep your confidences and are close friends, the people with whom you have developed a trusting relationship over the years. They are interested in what you are doing and want the best for you. They have been there for you when you have needed them, even without you having to ask, and you know you can rely on them to hold you up and

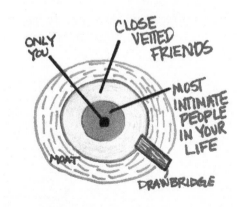

carry you through. They never talk poorly about you behind your back. (Note to self, everyone talks about everyone else when they aren't around, but friends only say nice things when you aren't there). You are in their circle of trust too, for the very same reasons.

Moving inward, in the dark gray circle, is where very intimate people in your life are allowed. These are the people you know you can count on for anything and will be there no matter what. These most intimate relationships are with the very few people who know most of your innermost secrets and love you unconditionally. For me, this is my husband and my sister. My children, although our love for each other is unconditional and I can trust them beyond reason, are not in this circle because I don't confide in them on things that are intimately personal. Trust me when I say they don't want to know these details.

In the innermost circle of your castle, the black circle, is where only for you reside. You are alone here because there are things that only you know. No one else has lived your life, and no other person on earth can understand completely what it is to be you. Try as you might, there aren't enough words in the English language nor enough time in life to explain each and every detail about you. And that is fine. It is as it should be.

MOST PEOPLE LIVE OUTSIDE THE WALLS

Most of the people in your life live outside the castle walls and beyond the moat. They aren't inside because they have not yet earned the right to be there.

They are fun to be with, you enjoy them, but you don't know if they are to be trusted with your needs and desires. If they earn the right, over time, by being trustworthy, the drawbridge is lowered to allow them passage.

Knowing these differences allows you to manage who you talk to about what and helps you avoid being hurt emotionally. Many times, due to the desire to have our group and our need to be worthy and belong, we are too quick to allow people into the light gray area. We let them in before we know they have our best interests at heart.

Or, because they are family, we allow them into our light gray or dark gray zones, thinking naively that they belong there. We must be vigilant about who belongs where. Many times, even family members need to be kept outside the moat. Just because they are family doesn't mean they belong in your circle of trust. But this also doesn't mean you need to cut them out completely. You just need to keep them at arm's length and your secrets to yourself.

YOU DECIDE WHERE PEOPLE BELONG

If you realize you let someone into your gray zones too early and, due to their behavior, they aren't eligible to be in your circle of trust, you can lower the drawbridge and return them to the space outside the moat. You need not say anything about this change; just know in your heart you are making it. The people outside the castle, beyond the moat, can be fun to be with. We can thoroughly enjoy their company, but we don't tell them intimate things or our hopes and dreams, and that is for the best. Instead, we can wave from the castle tower, smile and shout, "Hey, how's it going out there, do you want to go to dinner this Friday?"

This concept is good for all of us to understand and it is best taught at a young age because, desperate to have a special friend, young people go headfirst into their circle of trust, hand in hand with someone who has not been tested for fidelity and loyalty. Others let into young peoples' circle of trust too soon may talk behind their back, tell secret things they were supposed to keep in confidence, and wreak havoc on their heart. Young people don't understand how long it takes to develop deep friendships. They think just because the new buddy has a white dog like they do or that they are both in the same classroom it's a guaranteed basis for a long-lasting friendship. The importance of learning about the circle of trust helps all of us set boundaries and helps protect from having our heart hurt and our emotions triggered.

This idea doesn't work 100% of the time, but it is a good practice and helps us all know how to set boundaries and test-drive friendships in order to GET A GRIP.

ANALYZE YOUR CIRCLE OF TRUST

Our circle of trust is intended to protect us from being hurt and therefore triggered. A circle of trust works best when it contains only those we have vetted; and it is our responsibility to carefully set and maintain relationship boundaries.

Are there people within your castle who should be living beyond the moat? Have you allowed someone access too soon?

This process is not like social media where you must unfriend someone and then everyone knows. This analysis is for your eyes only and protects your heart without anyone being the wiser.

Who is in your light gray zone?

Who is in your dark gray zone?

TRACKING PROGRESS - WEEK TWELVE

CIRCLE OF TRUST							
ANALYZE WHO YOU HAVE IN YOUR CIRCLE OF TRUST. KEEP THOSE WHO COMPLETELY SUPPORT YOU AND WANT THE BEST FOR YOU. REMOVE THOSE WHO DON'T. REMEMBER JUST BECAUSE SOMEONE IS FAMILY OR HAS BEEN IN THE CIRCLE DOESN'T MEAN THEY GET TO REMAIN. ENJOY THEM FROM AFAR.							
	SUN	MON	TUES	WED	THUR	FRI	SAT
MAKE YOUR BED							
GRATITUDE/JOY JOURNAL							
CIRCLE OF TRUST							

Sunday through Saturday

Concentrate on who you friends are, and why.

Is there a friend who actually makes you feel badly about yourself?

Is there someone who always has to be one up?

Do you have a friend who only talks about themselves and never wants to listen to what you are doing?

As you work through each of your friends and acquaintances, determine if some should only be acquaintances.

Are there some that should be let go completely?

JOURNAL PAGE

13 WEEK SCHEDULE -WEEK TWELVE

CIRCLE OF TRUST							
ANALYZE WHO YOU HAVE IN YOUR CIRCLE OF TRUST. KEEP THOSE WHO COMPLETELY SUPPORT YOU AND WANT THE BEST FOR YOU. REMOVE THOSE WHO DON'T. REMEMBER JUST BECAUSE SOMEONE IS FAMILY OR HAS BEEN IN THE CIRCLE DOESN'T MEAN THEY GET TO REMAIN. ENJOY THEM FROM AFAR.							
	SUN	MON	TUES	WED	THUR	FRI	SAT
MAKE YOUR BED							
GRATITUDE/JOY JOURNAL							
CIRCLE OF TRUST							

GRATITUDES   JOY
MONDAY
1.   1.
2.   2.
3.   3.
4.   4.
5.   5.

TUESDAY
1.   1.
2.   2.
3.   3.
4.   4.
5.   5.

WEDNESDAY
1.   1.
2.   2.
3.   3.
4.   4.
5.   5.

THURSDAY
1.   1.
2.   2.
3.   3.
4.   4.
5.   5.

GRATITUDES   JOY
FRIDAY
1.   1.
2.   2.
3.   3.
4.   4.
5.   5.

SATURDAY
1.   1.
2.   2.
3.   3.
4.   4.
5.   5.

SUNDAY
1.   1.
2.   2.
3.   3.
4.   4.
5.   5.

MORE IN DEPTH TRACKING
SUNDAY THROUGH SATURDAY

CIRCLE OF TRUST							
ANALYZE WHO YOU HAVE IN YOUR CIRCLE OF TRUST. KEEP THOSE WHO COMPLETELY SUPPORT YOU AND WANT THE BEST FOR YOU. REMOVE THOSE WHO DON'T. REMEMBER JUST BECAUSE SOMEONE IS FAMILY OR HAS BEEN IN THE CIRCLE DOESN'T MEAN THEY GET TO REMAIN. ENJOY THEM FROM AFAR.							
	SUN	MON	TUES	WED	THUR	FRI	SAT
MAKE YOUR BED							
GRATITUDE/JOY JOURNAL							
CIRCLE OF TRUST							

Concentrate on who you are friends with, and why.

Is there a friend who actually makes you feel badly about yourself?

Is there someone who always has to be one up?

Analyze who belongs where.

FRIEND/ACQUAINTANCE	BEYOND THE MOAT?	LIGHT GRAY?	DARK GRAY?

XXI. WEEK THIRTEEN - MIND MAP

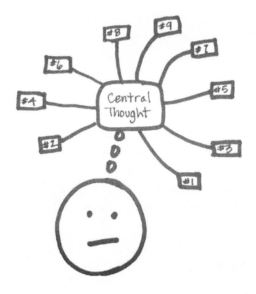

We can change the way that we think about external events,
even where we cannot change them.
Richard Koch

Because so much of what we think isn't true, we must train ourselves to choose the thoughts that work in our favor. We accomplish this by creating as many different thoughts as we can from the negative one we are thinking. Let's say you are thinking Cindy Lou Who/Dashing Dan has a fine life and you don't. In fact, you wish you were her/him and had her/his family and friends and life. You have been thinking this thought all day and it is making you cranky. Envy does that to us, and even worse, you are starting to take your cranky out on those nearest and dearest to you.

When you focus on one thought, what you were doing is called ruminating, which means you can't seem to think of anything other than the one thought, and when the thought is not a good one, and it is negative, it causes you grief. To GET A GRIP, STOP your thoughts in their tracks. Realize what you are doing, the thoughts you are thinking, and that you have no basis to prove anything. As a thought habit, ruminating on the negative is difficult to change, but you reprogram yourself over time, with effort, by creating positive new thoughts.

MIND MAP TO THINK BETTER THOUGHTS

Using my example above, once you catch yourself ruminating and have captured the negative thought(s) about Cindy Lou Who/Dashing Dan and how their life and friends are much better than yours, create as many different positive thoughts as you can. To make this work, be sure your new thoughts are true.

Examples of other positive thoughts you can think:

1. I have a good life

2. I am healthy

3. I have fun

4. My kids are silly and make me laugh

5. I love my husband

6. I have good friends

7. I like me

8. It is nice weather today

9. I am a good person

You can think any thoughts and as you make it to 9 or 10 you will notice you start to feel a sense of calm and you are happier.

Because we are wired a certain way, we can get stuck thinking repetitive thoughts and rumination can be our middle name. To stop this pattern of thought we can use a Mind Map to create thoughts centered on the positive, and what is true. Mind maps start with a center thought and then branch out to as many thoughts as you can think. They can be anything as long as they are positive and true.

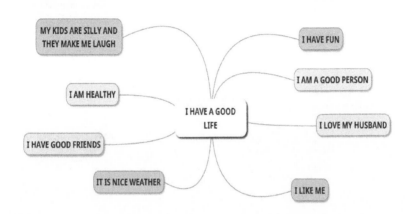

I found this mind mapping tool online and it's free. MindMup.com

This is an example of "I have a good life" rework.

From our example of driving down the road, someone cuts you off and you think "What a jerk".

To start the Mind Map the first thing to realize is your thought is negative. Negative thoughts don't benefit you.

Next question your thought, "Is that true?" Not necessarily.

I have driven in front of an unsuspecting driver and felt terrible about it because I just didn't see them. I am not a jerk and luckily I didn't cause an accident, but I am sure the person thought something along the lines of I am an idiot, mean, rude, etc. I am none of those things, but I am definitely at fault for not driving well.

Assuming someone does something intentionally with malice puts us on the defense and full of feeling like everyone is bad. Without evidence of such things, isn't it better that we come up with other thoughts that might be true and that make us feel much better about humanity?

Let's use a mind map to rework the "What A Jerk" example.

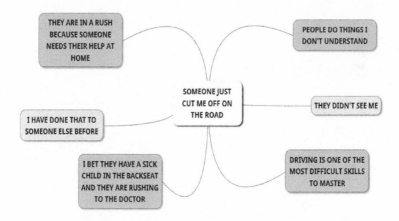

Read through the alternate thoughts that you can think. As you think thoughts other than, "What a jerk," you start to calm down and feel better.

TRACKING PROGRESS - WEEK THIRTEEN

MIND MAP							
WHEN YOU GET FIXATED ON ONE THOUGHT, STOP, BREATHE, AND TAKE TIME TO THINK AS MANY OTHER THOUGHTS AS YOU CAN, WHICH ARE BASED ON POSITIVITY AND TRUTH.							
	SUN	MON	TUES	WED	THUR	FRI	SAT
MAKE YOUR BED							
GRATITUDE/JOY JOURNAL							
MIND MAP							

Sunday through Saturday

Each day practice changing your thoughts to those that work well for you. Change each negative, fear based, worried thought into as many other positive, forward thinking, excited thoughts as you can.

JOURNAL PAGE

13 WEEK SCHEDULE -WEEK THIRTEEN

MIND MAP							
WHEN YOU GET FIXATED ON ONE THOUGHT, STOP, BREATHE, AND TAKE TIME TO THINK AS MANY OTHER THOUGHTS AS YOU CAN, WHICH ARE BASED ON POSITIVITY AND TRUTH.							
	SUN	MON	TUES	WED	THUR	FRI	SAT
MAKE YOUR BED							
GRATITUDE/JOY JOURNAL							
MIND MAP							

GRATITUDES   JOY

MONDAY
1.   1.
2.   2.
3.   3.
4.   4.
5.   5.

TUESDAY
1.   1.
2.   2.
3.   3.
4.   4.
5.   5.

WEDNESDAY
1.   1.
2.   2.
3.   3.
4.   4.
5.   5.

THURSDAY
1.   1.
2.   2.
3.   3.
4.   4.
5.   5.

GRATITUDES   JOY

FRIDAY
1.   1.
2.   2.
3.   3.
4.   4.
5.   5.

SATURDAY
1.   1.
2.   2.
3.   3.
4.   4.
5.   5.

SUNDAY
1.   1.
2.   2.
3.   3.
4.   4.
5.   5.

MORE IN DEPTH TRACKING
SUNDAY THROUGH SATURDAY

MIND MAP							
WHEN YOU GET FIXATED ON ONE THOUGHT, STOP, BREATHE, AND TAKE TIME TO THINK AS MANY OTHER THOUGHTS AS YOU CAN, WHICH ARE BASED ON POSITIVITY AND TRUTH.							
	SUN	MON	TUES	WED	THUR	FRI	SAT
MAKE YOUR BED							
GRATITUDE/JOY JOURNAL							
MIND MAP							

Each day practice changing your thoughts to those that work well for you. Change each negative, fear based, worried thought into as many other positive, forward thinking, excited thoughts as you can.

SUNDAY

NEGATIVE THOUGHT =	
OTHER POSITIVE FORWARD-THINKING THOUGHTS	

MONDAY

NEGATIVE THOUGHT =	
OTHER POSITIVE FORWARD-THINKING THOUGHTS	

TUESDAY

NEGATIVE THOUGHT =	
OTHER POSITIVE FORWARD-THINKING THOUGHTS	

WEDNESDAY

NEGATIVE THOUGHT =	
OTHER POSITIVE FORWARD-THINKING THOUGHTS	

THURSDAY

NEGATIVE THOUGHT =	
OTHER POSITIVE FORWARD-THINKING THOUGHTS	

FRIDAY

NEGATIVE THOUGHT =	
OTHER POSITIVE FORWARD-THINKING THOUGHTS	

SATURDAY

NEGATIVE THOUGHT =	
OTHER POSITIVE FORWARD-THINKING THOUGHTS	

XXII.   SIX WEEK JOURNAL PAGES

If you have chosen to follow the six-week schedule, and I highly recommend this one to start with, the following journaling pages will be your guide.

You will use the suggestions for what to track from each of the chapters IX – XXI which I have included on the following pages.

If you would like to you can use the more in-depth tracking pages. I recommend using these for the topics that need the most work.

The six-week schedule is:

Week One- Catch Yourself Thinking, Hearing the self-talk in your head, Is What I Am Thinking True?

Week Two - Negative Repetitive Thinking, Limiting Beliefs

Week Three - Fear, Worry, And Then What?

Week Four - Judging - Ourselves and others, Am I?

Week Five - Triggers, Planning Ahead, Circle of Trust

Week Six - Mind Mapping

WEEK ONE

CATCH YOURSELF THINKING

Sunday – In contrast to what so many believe, our old DNA brain runs one task at a time and does not multitask. As you focus on your thoughts, only work on catching yourself thinking. Ignore all other distractions.

Monday – Take responsibility for your thinking. As you focus on catching yourself thinking, avoid judgement of your thoughts.

Tuesday – As you notice your thoughts, write notes on the type of thoughts you are thinking. Are they worries, fears, judgments? Are they negative? Create a labeling system for the type of thoughts you think, and after several days of recording, look for patterns.

Wednesday – As you notice your thoughts today, are they productive? Or just noise?

Thursday – As you gain confidence catching your thinking, you can start to analyze if what you tend to think is true. Are you holding onto your beliefs with a death grip? Could you loosen your grasp and change your thought patterns to truly GET A GRIP?

Friday – Do you tend to notice the good things that happen to you or more so the bad?

Saturday – Do you focus your thoughts on what you want? Or on what you don't want?

THE VOICE IN YOUR HEAD

Sunday through Saturday

In the same way you learned to catch yourself thinking, check to see what the voice in your head is saying.

At each of your scheduled check in times, note what message you are sending yourself.

Is it positive?

True?

Joyous?

IS THAT TRUE?

Sunday – Are you honest with yourself about how you spend your time? Do you analyze what you do and when you do it? Check your weekly schedule and look at how you spend your time, then ask yourself if that is in line with what you thought you were doing.

Monday – As you head out to do what you do on Monday; what are you thinking? Are you thinking today will be hard? Are you worried that your supervisor is mad? Whichever thoughts you are creating in your mind, be sure to prove them correct or false.

Tuesday – As you make it through day two of this week, look for patterns in your thinking. Are you often wrong in your assumptions? Remember to ask "is that true" to clarify if what you read, hear or think is false.

Wednesday – This is hump day, or is it? When thinking through this commonly held view of a Wednesday, are we making assumptions about every person's work week? Even simple thoughts need some attention, don't they?

Thursday – Do you read emails from friends, acquaintances, or co-workers that quote a statistic or contain an opinion and stop to question "is that true?" If you don't, today is a great day to start.

Friday – As you complete five days of Think GET A GRIP work, review your actions and how you go about accomplishing tasks and ask yourself, how can I do better? How can I be more efficient? And is my opinion of how well I am doing true? Does it work in my favor?

Saturday – Host a family/friend meeting to learn if how you believe things are going is actually how others in your family/friend group feel. "Is that true" questions work in all sorts of situations

6 WEEK SCHEDULE -WEEK ONE

	SUN	MON	TUES	WED	THUR	FRI	SAT
MAKE YOUR BED							
GRATITUDE JOURNALING							
CATCH YOURSELF THINKING							
SELF TALK							
IS THAT TRUE?							

GRATITUDES   JOY
MONDAY
1.   1.
2.   2.
3.   3.
4.   4.
5.   5.

TUESDAY
1.   1.
2.   2.
3.   3.
4.   4.
5.   5.

WEDNESDAY
1.   1.
2.   2.
3.   3.
4.   4.
5.   5.

THURSDAY
1.   1.
2.   2.
3.   3.
4.   4.
5.   5.

GRATITUDES   JOY
FRIDAY
1.   1.
2.   2.
3.   3.
4.   4.
5.   5.

SATURDAY
1.   1.
2.   2.
3.   3.
4.   4.
5.   5.

SUNDAY
1.   1.
2.   2.
3.   3.
4.   4.
5.   5.

WEEK TWO

NEGATIVE THINKING

Sunday through Saturday

Chart whether your thoughts are negative, neutral, or positive. You can use something like what I provided below.

Look for patterns of time or situations which cause you to have a negative focus. At the end of the week, look at times of day, and what was happening to understand what irritates you so in the future you will be able to prepare mentally and emotionally for upcoming experiences.

	MORNING	Thoughts are Negative/ Neutral/ Positive?	NOON	Thoughts are Negative/ Neutral/ Positive?	NIGHT	Thoughts are Negative/ Neutral/ Positive?
Sunday						
Monday						
Tuesday						
Wednesday						
Thursday						
Friday						
Saturday						

LIMITING BELIEFS

Sunday through Saturday

Each day as you make decisions try to get to the bottom of what made you decide the way you did. Was there a limiting belief driving your thoughts in a particular direction? When you locate your limiting beliefs, start making a list and then prove them wrong when necessary.

6 WEEK SCHEDULE -WEEK TWO

	SUN	MON	TUES	WED	THUR	FRI	SAT
MAKE YOUR BED							
GRATITUDE JOURNALING							
NEGATIVE THINKING							
LIMITING BELIEFS							

GRATITUDES JOY

MONDAY
1.   1.
2.   2.
3.   3.
4.   4.
5.   5.

TUESDAY
1.   1.
2.   2.
3.   3.
4.   4.
5.   5.

WEDNESDAY
1.   1.
2.   2.
3.   3.
4.   4.
5.   5.

THURSDAY
1.   1.
2.   2.
3.   3.
4.   4.
5.   5.

GRATITUDES JOY

FRIDAY
1.   1.
2.   2.
3.   3.
4.   4.
5.   5.

SATURDAY
1.   1.
2.   2.
3.   3.
4.   4.
5.   5.

SUNDAY
1.   1.
2.   2.
3.   3.
4.   4.
5.   5.

WEEK THREE

FEAR

Sunday through Saturday

Write down your fears when they occur. Note them on your phone or in some way that you can see the entire list at the end of the week. After seven days, review the things that make you afraid. Are they real? Or are they things based on your thoughts of What If?

Each time you feel fearful, ask yourself if it is something you created in your head, if it is truly fear, or could it be excitement.

Fear is a large obstacle to overcome in order to GET A GRIP because it drives most of our negative thought processes. One of our biggest fears is that we aren't in control. When we are organized, we aren't caught off guard, we know what is coming, and we have what we need when we need it. We don't feel the need to fear that we won't be ready.

WORRY

Sunday through Saturday

Each time you note you are worrying, and especially for each episode of extended worry, use the "And Then What" exercise to work through your thoughts.

To recoup the time we lose by worrying, we must go all the way down the hall, open the door, look behind it, and walk through to the other side. Once there, we must get to know our worries well, work through them, and realize they will not be the end of us.

6 WEEK SCHEDULE-WEEK THREE

	SUN	MON	TUES	WED	THUR	FRI	SAT
MAKE YOUR BED							
GRATITUDE JOURNALING							
FEAR							
WORRY/AND THEN WHAT							

GRATITUDES   JOY

MONDAY
1.   1.
2.   2.
3.   3.
4.   4.
5.   5.

TUESDAY
1.   1.
2.   2.
3.   3.
4.   4.
5.   5.

WEDNESDAY
1.   1.
2.   2.
3.   3.
4.   4.
5.   5.

THURSDAY
1.   1.
2.   2.
3.   3.
4.   4.
5.   5.

GRATITUDES   JOY

FRIDAY
1.   1.
2.   2.
3.   3.
4.   4.
5.   5.

SATURDAY
1.   1.
2.   2.
3.   3.
4.   4.
5.   5.

SUNDAY
1.   1.
2.   2.
3.   3.
4.   4.
5.   5.

WEEK FOUR

JUDGING

Sunday through Saturday

Each time you judge yourself or others, ask yourself for proof of your thoughts, and make sure you know of what you speak

To motivate real change, you can charge yourself one dollar for each time you judge yourself or others. Get immediate feedback by giving that dollar to someone around you so that you feel the impact of judgment. In this way, you can train yourself to stop being judgmental and free your thoughts to be more positive.

AM I?

Sunday through Saturday

Each day focus on your decisions and actions and note if they are in line with your goals for yourself, or are you doing what you imagine others desire from you?

Are you pleasing yourself?

Are you exercising self-care?

Are you setting goals and doing your best work?

Or are you a people pleaser first and putting yourself last?

6 WEEK SCHEDULE-WEEK FOUR

	SUN	MON	TUES	WED	THUR	FRI	SAT
MAKE YOUR BED							
GRATITUDE JOURNALING							
JUDGING							
AM I?							

GRATITUDES   JOY   GRATITUDES   JOY

MONDAY   **FRIDAY**
1.   1.   1.   1.
2.   2.   2.   2.
3.   3.   3.   3.
4.   4.   4.   4.
5.   5.   5.   5.

TUESDAY   **SATURDAY**
1.   1.   1.   1.
2.   2.   2.   2.
3.   3.   3.   3.
4.   4.   4.   4.
5.   5.   5.   5.

WEDNESDAY   **SUNDAY**
1.   1.   1.   1.
2.   2.   2.   2.
3.   3.   3.   3.
4.   4.   4.   4.
5.   5.   5.   5.

THURSDAY
1.   1.
2.   2.
3.   3.
4.   4.
5.   5.

WEEK FIVE

TRIGGERS

Sunday through Saturday

Each time you react in a big way, whether silently or aloud, note what triggered you. Stop immediately and really concentrate on the emotion coursing through your veins. Learn the basis for what you are feeling. These are your triggers.

When you start to feel emotions building, stop, and breathe. Breathe deeply, slowly in, and slowly out. Count to 4 slowly while breathing in, hold your breath for 4 counts, and then let your breath out for four counts. Concentrate on slowing your heart rate and only focus on your breathing. Once you can do four counts, the next goal is to do it for 8.

PLAN AHEAD

Sunday through Saturday

Take time this week to set a schedule that works for you. Make sure to check and see if what you agree to do and what you say yes to is actually just you trying to belong which zaps your energy and joy.

Pay close attention to where and how you spend your time. Often, we spend time doing things we don't enjoy and forget to take care of ourselves. Plan times for self-care and rejuvenation.

Look for days and times in your schedule which will trigger your emotions. Use your list of possible reactions to emotions especially when you know you will be triggered. Pay attention to how you feel physically because triggered emotions are first felt in our body.

CIRCLE OF TRUST

Sunday through Saturday

Concentrate on who you friends are, and why.

Is there a friend who actually makes you feel badly about yourself?

Is there someone who always has to be one up?

Do you have a friend who only talks about themselves and never wants to listen to what you are doing?

As you work through each of your friends and acquaintances, determine if some should only be acquaintances.

Are there some that should be let go completely?

6 WEEK SCHEDULE - WEEK FIVE

	SUN	MON	TUES	WED	THUR	FRI	SAT
MAKE YOUR BED							
GRATITUDE JOURNALING							
TRIGGERS							
PLANNING AHEAD							
CIRCLE OF TRUST							

GRATITUDES   JOY

MONDAY
1.   1.
2.   2.
3.   3.
4.   4.
5.   5.

TUESDAY
1.   1.
2.   2.
3.   3.
4.   4.
5.   5.

WEDNESDAY
1.   1.
2.   2.
3.   3.
4.   4.
5.   5.

THURSDAY
1.   1.
2.   2.
3.   3.
4.   4.
5.   5.

GRATITUDES   JOY

FRIDAY
1.   1.
2.   2.
3.   3.
4.   4.
5.   5.

SATURDAY
1.   1.
2.   2.
3.   3.
4.   4.
5.   5.

SUNDAY
1.   1.
2.   2.
3.   3.
4.   4.
5.   5.

WEEK SIX

MIND MAPPING

Sunday through Saturday

Each day practice changing your thoughts to those that work well for you. Change each negative, fear based, worried thought into as many other positive, forward thinking, excited thoughts as you can.

6 WEEK SCHEDULE - WEEK SIX

	SUN	MON	TUES	WED	THUR	FRI	SAT
MAKE YOUR BED							
GRATITUDE JOURNALING							
MIND MAPPING							

GRATITUDES   JOY

MONDAY
1.   1.
2.   2.
3.   3.
4.   4.
5.   5.

TUESDAY
1.   1.
2.   2.
3.   3.
4.   4.
5.   5.

WEDNESDAY
1.   1.
2.   2.
3.   3.
4.   4.
5.   5.

THURSDAY
1.   1.
2.   2.
3.   3.
4.   4.
5.   5.

GRATITUDES   JOY

FRIDAY
1.   1.
2.   2.
3.   3.
4.   4.
5.   5.

SATURDAY
1.   1.
2.   2.
3.   3.
4.   4.
5.   5.

SUNDAY
1.   1.
2.   2.
3.   3.
4.   4.
5.   5.

XXIII.   NOW PUT IT ALL TOGETHER

Knowledge comes by taking things apart, analysis.
But wisdom comes by putting things together.
John Alexander Morrison

When you get done doing this heavy work, I want you to return to the table of contents and read it as the bullet points of what I wanted you to learn. You can also use this list as a reminder of what you are working on for yourself. And this list is a starting place for learning other valuable mental wellness tips.

I want to reiterate that counseling is the best gift you can give yourself. But it is expensive so do what you can. Many insurance companies cover a specific number of visits each year. Finding the right person for you is wonderful, but even if you don't gel with the therapist, you can still glean nuggets of truth. And if you happen to find someone that resonates with you, stick with them for as long as you can to work on your goals. This book is based on Cognitive Behavioral Therapy techniques and I like meeting with counselors who specialize in CBT.

Most of what we think comes from our old DNA so don't beat yourself up for having the same train of thought, it is to be expected. Just continue to do the work and you will notice a gradual change.

The Voice In Your Head needs to be managed in more ways than controlling the negative messages it likes to send. We must learn to quiet the negative self-talk in our head to allow us to state our needs and to voice our opinions. To reach our happy place we need to have our needs met and we can't do that unless we state what they are. And those around us benefit from hearing what we believe and what we think is valuable and true. And we benefit from hearing the same from others. Don't talk yourself into being afraid to speak up.

GET A GRIP, which essentially is self-awareness and mental wellness, is vital to reaching your promise and potential. And part of mental wellness involves exercise. I heard you groan, and I get it. But hear me out. Even getting slightly sweaty helps immensely. Especially when you are feeling anxious, a brisk long walk can and does work wonders.

Being outside in natural surroundings, while on your walk, is a quick fix to feeling overwhelmed. If you live near the ocean, sitting on the beach and realizing the enormity of the water on our planet helps put things in perspective. And if you live in the mountains, you can accomplish the same understanding by hiking to what appears close, but once started on your way you realize it is really far away. And if you have ever driven across the prairies, you know all too well how vast a distance is. Noticing the enormity in nature helps put our problems into perspective. And when we experience the beauty in nature our level of compassion is raised. All of these things help us maintain our grip on mental wellness.

And just know medication can work wonders and it doesn't have to be taken forever. When I retired from day-to-day education, it hit me hard. I realized I was being super crabby, and I felt angry with the world. I went back to counseling and I used medication because I knew I needed a little something to help me get through the depression. It isn't forever, but it is for when needed.

Finally, working on our own circle of trust demands that we analyze what type of friend we are to others. Are we overbearing, self-centered, untrustworthy, or in it to win it?

Now having completed one round of the work, you can work on all the skills each day and keep track of which ones give you the most trouble. Some will be easier than others but as you move to your next round of doing this work try focusing on all the skills together. Then once you notice the ones that give you the most grief you can zero in on those. The two that I focus on for me are "Is That True?" and Mind Mapping.

Here are two tracking sheets you can use more easily now that you have gone through the work. One is for the thirteen-week schedule and the other for the six-week schedule.

THIRTEEN WEEK SCHEDULE

WEEK	WORK	SUN	MON	TUES	WED	THUR	FRI	SAT
	13 WEEK PROGRESS MONITORING							
1	MAKE YOUR BED							
	GRATITUDE JOURNALING							
	CATCH YOURSELF THINKING							
2	MAKE YOUR BED							
	GRATITUDE JOURNALING							
	SELF TALK							
3	MAKE YOUR BED							
	GRATITUDE JOURNALING							
	IS THAT TRUE?							
4	MAKE YOUR BED							
	GRATITUDE JOURNALING							
	NEGATIVE THINKING							
5	MAKE YOUR BED							
	GRATITUDE JOURNALING							
	LIMITING BELIEFS							
6	MAKE YOUR BED							
	GRATITUDE JOURNALING							
	FEAR							
7	MAKE YOUR BED							
	GRATITUDE JOURNALING							
	WORRY/AND THEN WHAT							
8	MAKE YOUR BED							
	GRATITUDE JOURNALING							
	JUDGING							
9	MAKE YOUR BED							
	GRATITUDE JOURNALING							
	AM I?							
10	MAKE YOUR BED							
	GRATITUDE JOURNALING							
	TRIGGERS							
11	MAKE YOUR BED							
	GRATITUDE JOURNALING							
	PLANNING AHEAD							
12	MAKE YOUR BED							
	GRATITUDE JOURNALING							
	CIRCLE OF TRUST							
13	MAKE YOUR BED							
	GRATITUDE JOURNALING							
	MIND MAPPING							

SIX WEEK SCHEDULE

6 WEEK PROGRESS MONITORING								
WEEK	WORK	SUN	MON	TUES	WED	THUR	FRI	SAT
1	MAKE YOUR BED							
	GRATITUDE JOURNALING							
	CATCH YOURSELF THINKING							
	SELF TALK							
	IS THAT TRUE?							
2	MAKE YOUR BED							
	GRATITUDE JOURNALING							
	NEGATIVE THINKING							
	LIMITING BELIEFS							
3	MAKE YOUR BED							
	GRATITUDE JOURNALING							
	FEAR							
	WORRY/AND THEN WHAT							
4	MAKE YOUR BED							
	GRATITUDE JOURNALING							
	JUDGING							
	AM I?							
5	MAKE YOUR BED							
	GRATITUDE JOURNALING							
	TRIGGERS							
	PLANNING AHEAD							
	CIRCLE OF TRUST							
6	MAKE YOUR BED							
	GRATITUDE JOURNALING							
	MIND MAPPING							

You have read my words so I have a few favors to ask.

1. Please let me know if what I have taught in this book is helpful to you, and if so, how. I want to be able to share what each of us does to GET A GRIP so others can benefit from what we have learned.

2. I want you to always remember that it is normal to worry, etc., but it is not mandatory - you can change your thinking if you truly want to.

3. Please share your strategies with your loved ones, especially with your children (if you have them) so they understand they struggle just like other people do and can learn to GET A GRIP.

4. Offer details of your GET A GRIP journey with others, when appropriate, so they can know working on their mental health is normal - everyone does it to some degree.

And please know, in your heart, my greatest hope is you will work on your mental health to a high degree so that you can GET A GRIP and reach your promise and potential.

XXIV.   EPILOGUE/CONCLUSION

*Emotion is welded to everything we think. We
use images of the past to create the emotions
we need now in order to support our goal
directed behavior.*

Russell Markley, PhD

We must make our years on earth good now, rather than waking one day with regret and hindsight about what we wished we would have done. I call this living by the deathbed. This sounds awful, but it isn't. What I mean when I say this is that I make decisions based on whether or not I will have regret while I lie on my deathbed. This way of thinking helps me overcome my fear and worry so I can take advantage of opportunities that come my way.

For sure, we want to live a life that is good to look back on, and we also want to live a life that is fun planning for in the future, but don't we want to especially enjoy the life we are living right now? We want our cake and eat it too, right?

Negative mind tapes hinder us from enjoying what we've done, what we plan to do, and most especially, the present moment. To think in the best way possible, live a life that is worthy of living, one that fills us with joy, and to have meaning in our existence, we must avoid the proverbial checklist of "shoulds", what is right and what is cool. We must search for what matters to us, what values we hold, and what meets our own needs. We must live up to our own standards.

We think too much about what does not matter, worry about things that never happen and spend too little time contemplating the ideas that can help us master our lives. I wasted a lot of time worrying about things that never happened, and the things that did occur, I never in my wildest dreams (or nightmares!) considered. Learning to overcome needless worry frees us to live fully in the now. Life demands our best, and to be ready, we must be in the right mindset to GET A GRIP.

Although doing this work without medication is my first desire, there are times when my strategies alone aren't enough. If you are there, please do what it takes to be well. Practice every one of my strategies until they become second nature and develop ones of your own. Take medication if you need to, and I absolutely want you to seek professional help. Counseling, like any prescribed doctor appointments, is absolutely necessary to maintaining our mental health.

Bottom line, revel in the knowledge that you are here for a reason, you are loved as you are, you can work to reach your promise and potential, and we all need you to share your special gifts with the world.

BIBLIOGRAPHY

I have learned so much from so many on my GET A GRIP journey. After some initial introductions to what it means to think well, and counseling, I read many wonderful books, attended seminars, and took classes to learn so much more. I firmly believe when you want to improve anything, but especially mindset, you need to gain knowledge from people in the know. All of my reading and learning helped me develop my strategies that I have shared with you. I've compiled a list of some of my favorites, in no particular order, except the first one is my all-time favorite. They are packed with great knowledge, are easy to read and understand, and offer advice that is easy to implement. If you are purchasing any of these books, please support me by using my links below.

Tolle, E. (2005). *A New Earth: Awakening to Your Life's Purpose.* New York, NY: Penguin
Purchase at https://amzn.to/2EoNxRY

Seligman, M. E. P. (2006) *Learned Optimism: How to Change Your Mind and Your Life.* New York, NY: Pocket Books.
Purchase at https://amzn.to/2U2SsNU

Russell, B. (1930). *The Conquest of Happiness.* New York, NY: Liveright
Purchase at https://amzn.to/34yK3I8

Seigel, D. Bryson, T. (2011). *The Whole-Brain Child: 12 Revolutionary Strategies to Nurture Your Child's Developing Mind.* New York: Random House
Purchase at https://amzn.to/2UkfNgH

Keltner, D. (2009). *Born To Be Good: The Science of a Meaningful Life.* New York, NY: W. W. Norton
Purchase at https://amzn.to/3eeWM71

Manson, M. (2016). *The Subtle Art Of Not Giving a F*ck: A Counterintuitive Approach To Living A Good Life*. New York, NY: HarperCollins
Purchase at https://amzn.to/2GVHDJH

Mellin, L. (2003). *The Pathway*. New York, NY: HarperCollins
Purchase at https://amzn.to/2yQNePy

Greenberger, D. Padesky, C. (2016). *Mind Over Mood: Change How You Feel by Changing The Way You Think*. New York, NY: Guilford
Purchase at https://amzn.to/2VduSOp

Cabane, O. (2012). *The Charisma Myth: How Anyone Can Master the Art and Science of Personal Magnetism*. New York, NY: Penguin
Purchase at https://amzn.to/2Oix4n6

Everyone is Free (to wear sunscreen) listen to the song here https://youtu.be/ZxEHGAY7LbY

If you buy something via these links, I may earn an affiliate commission.

ACKNOWLEDGMENTS

I want to thank every student for the privilege of spending my days with you, you are the young people who are the hope of tomorrow, and who inspired me to write down the things I taught you so others can learn them too. And thank you to your parents for allowing me to work with their children.

A huge thank you goes to my first editors, Candace Patrick, and Elizabeth Morris, who without their help and perseverance this book would not exist. It is difficult to get someone to stay focused on your book that means so much to you and yet these two did just that.

My husband deserves a medal for putting up with my need to sequester myself in my office and not come up for air for hours. Thank you goes to him from the bottom of my heart for supporting my desire to write this book.

Thank you to Parker Murray for helping me with illustrations and designing the cover of the book. His talent and ability to scrutinize were invaluable.

A thank you goes to Cindy Draughon, the editor I hired from Fiverr.com, who put the final editing on my book. If ever in need she is a great resource.

And a debt of appreciation to my Beta readers, friend Larry, sister Candy, daughter Elizabeth and husband John. Their willingness to be critical and offer suggestions made the book more readable and entertaining.

A shout out goes to Brett Hatcher, a childhood friend, who helped me keep going by asking multiple times, "how is that book coming along?"

I wish I could personally thank Larry the counselor and other people who have taught me so much over the years. They were instrumental in adding to my understanding of thinking patterns and what to do to improve mine and with that knowledge help others improve theirs.

And the biggest of thanks goes to you, the reader. Thank you very much for purchasing my book. I would love to hear how it helped you. Please, drop me a note.

And last but not least, we change the world for the better by changing ourselves so thank you for working on your skills and mindset to make the world a better place. And if you have children, please teach them these skills while they are young to ensure their future is bright.

CONNECT WITH HEATHER

EMAIL

thinkgetagrip@gmail.com

SOCIAL MEDIA

Facebook

FB thinkgetagrip

Instagram

Instagram – ThinkGetAGrip

Twitter

Twitter – RaiseGoodHumans

WEBSITES

www.raisinggoodhumans.com

www.thinkgetagrip.com

When life tries to test your fuse length,

grab your shirt collar and say to yourself

GET A GRIP!

Then stand tall and keep on truckin'.

You've got this.

Made in the USA
Las Vegas, NV
25 May 2021

23621219R00152